Pocket
KUALA LUMPUR
TOP SIGHTS · LOCAL LIFE · MADE EASY

D1637767

Isabel Albiston

526 206 29 7

In This Book

QuickStart Guide

Your keys to understanding the city – we help you decide what to do and how to do it

Need to Know
Tips for a smooth trip

Neighbourhoods
What's where

Explore Kuala Lumpur

The best things to see and do, neighbourhood by neighbourhood

Top Sights
Make the most of your visit

Local Life
The insider's city

The Best of Kuala Lumpur

The city's highlights in handy lists to help you plan

Best Walks
See the city on foot

Kuala Lumpur's Best...
The best experiences

Survival Guide

Tips and tricks for a seamless, hassle-free city experience

Getting Around
Travel like a local

Essential Information
Including where to stay

Our selection of the city's best places to eat, drink and experience:

◎ **Sights**

❎ **Eating**

🍸 **Drinking**

⭐ **Entertainment**

🔒 **Shopping**

These symbols give you the vital information for each listing:

- ☏ Telephone Numbers
- ⊙ Opening Hours
- P Parking
- @ Internet Access
- 📶 Wi-Fi Access
- 🥗 Vegetarian Selection
- 📖 English-Language Menu
- 👪 Family-Friendly
- 🚌 Bus
- ⛴ Ferry
- Ⓛ LRT
- 🚝 Monorail
- 🚆 Train

Find each listing quickly on maps for each neighbourhood:

Bar Hemingway

16 🍸 Map p233, B2

Legend has it that Hemi self, wielding a machine erate this timber-pan ered bar during showpiece is a en by Papa ar town. Dress s.com; Hôtel Rit ; ⊙6.30pm-2a

Lonely Planet's Kuala Lumpur

Lonely Planet Pocket Guides are designed to get you straight to the heart of the city.

Inside you'll find all the must-see sights, plus tips to make your visit to each one really memorable. We've split the city into easy-to-navigate neighbourhoods and provided clear maps so you'll find your way around with ease. Our expert authors have searched out the best of the city: walks, food, nightlife and shopping, to name a few. Because you want to explore, our 'Local Life' pages will take you to some of the most exciting areas to experience the real Kuala Lumpur.

And of course you'll find all the practical tips you need for a smooth trip: itineraries for short visits, how to get around, and how much to tip the guy who serves you a drink at the end of a long day's exploration.

It's your guarantee of a really great experience.

Our Promise

You can trust our travel information because Lonely Planet authors visit the places we write about, each and every edition. We never accept freebies for positive coverage, so you can rely on us to tell it like it is.

QuickStart Guide 7

Explore Kuala Lumpur 21

Worth a Trip:

QuickStart Guide

Welcome to Kuala Lumpur

Glitzy malls rub shoulders with street markets, gleaming skyscrapers loom over colonial buildings, and world-class restaurants vie for patronage with bustling open-air satay stands: Kuala Lumpur may be racing toward the future, but its rich cultural heritage refuses to be left behind. From steaming bowls of *asam laksa* to sinfully sweet morsels of *kueh,* the very best part is its legendary food.

KLCC Park (p25)
TOOYKRUB / SHUTTERSTOCK ©

Kuala Lumpur Top Sights

Petronas Towers (p24)

It's impossible to resist the magnetic allure of these 452m-high structures, the embodiment of Malaysia's transformation into a modern nation. The views both from and of the towers are equally riveting.

Tun Abdul Razak Heritage Park (p94)

Better known as the Lake Gardens, this is KL's major recreational park, with a day's worth of sights including botanical gardens, a bird park, and a number of worthwhile museums surrounding the greenery.

Islamic Arts Museum (p96)

This terrific museum highlights the diversity of art – from miniature paintings to interior design – and the richness of regional variation in the Islamic world: from the Middle East, through China, India and Southeast Asia.

Merdeka Square (p54)

There is nowhere better in KL to soak up its British colonial past, including its Mughal-inspired architecture, than around this former cricket green where in 1957 independence was declared and the Malaysian flag raised for the first time.

Batu Caves (p88)

In these soaring limestone caves – the country's top Hindu pilgrimage site – intricate geological formations compete for your attention with colourful shrines and psychedelic dioramas.

Thean Hou Temple (p114)

The glorious sunsets over the city, and the devotional atmosphere during Chinese festival times, draw visitors to this massive, fantastically gaudy Chinese temple atop Robson Hill.

Menara Kuala Lumpur (p26)

Rival to the Petronas Towers for glorious city views, this 421m-high telecommunications tower is best approached via the canopy walkway of the KL Forest Eco Park.

Sri Mahamariamman Temple (p56)

The entrance to this venerable Hindu shrine – the oldest in Malaysia – is crowned by a five-tiered *gopuram* (temple tower), covered in riotously colourful statues of Hindu deities.

Forest Research Institute Malaysia (FRIM; p90)

A natural escape from KL's urban grind, this 600-hectare forest reserve has hiking trails and quiet lanes for biking. The highlight is a fabulous canopy walkway.

Kuala Lumpur Local Life

Insider tips to help you find the real cit

In KL, the traditional greeting is *'Sudah makan?'* (Have you eaten yet?); hawker stal and *kopitiam* (coffee shops) are where locals catch up on gossip. Everyone can find their tribe in KL's diverse neighbourhoods, from mall-goers to foodies, street photog raphers and coffee aficionados.

Brickfields Temples & Treats (p98)

▶ Indian eateries
▶ Colourful temples

From bright lights and colourful shrines to blaring Tamil pop tunes and the scents of frying spices and jasmine garlands, KL's official Little India is sensory overloaded. Experience this multicultural neighbourhood like the locals who live here by eating at their favourite food stalls and visiting their places of worship.

Pudu (p50)

▶ Street food
▶ Urban exploration

Hankering for the flavours of Chinatown without the crowds? Visit this laid-back Chinese neighbourhood, with some of KL's most charming pockets of shophouses and lip-smackingly good street eats. The sprawling Pudu wet market is one of the city's biggest and most lively.

A Taste of Bukit Bintang (p28)

▶ Street food
▶ Bars

More than anything else, the search for the next great meal is what makes this city tick. Street food is an obsession, but in Bukit Bintang you can see how the experience has been moved indoors without compromising c atmosphere (much).

Boutique-Hopping in Bangsar Baru (p116)

▶ Shopping
▶ Restaurants

Come for the shopping, stay for the food. Or do the reverse in this buzzing suburban enclave brimming with fashionable cafes, a diverse selec tion of restaurants and cutting-edge boutiques run by up-and-coming local designers.

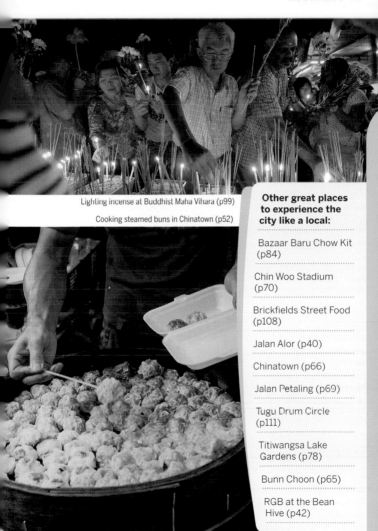

Lighting incense at Buddhist Maha Vihara (p99)

Cooking steamed buns in Chinatown (p52)

Other great places to experience the city like a local:

Bazaar Baru Chow Kit (p84)

Chin Woo Stadium (p70)

Brickfields Street Food (p108)

Jalan Alor (p40)

Chinatown (p66)

Jalan Petaling (p69)

Tugu Drum Circle (p111)

Titiwangsa Lake Gardens (p78)

Bunn Choon (p65)

RGB at the Bean Hive (p42)

Kuala Lumpur Day Planner

Day One

Head to the Kuala Lumpur City Centre (KLCC), where you've prebooked tickets up the **Petronas Towers** (p24). Afterwards, browse the shops in **Suria KLCC** (p47) and see a free art exhibition at the excellent **Galeri Petronas** (p33). Join local office workers for a vegetarian lunch at the **Dharma Realm Guan Yin Sagely Monastery** (p36), or eat at one of the restaurants at Suria KLCC.

Take a post-lunch stroll around **KLCC Park** (p25), admiring the view of the towers, then take a look at contemporary Malaysian art at the **ILHAM** (p32) in the Foster + Partners–designed tower. Join the 3pm tour of the Malay-style wooden house **Rumah Penghulu Abu Seman** (p33) next to Badan Warisan Malaysia, or learn about sea life at **Aquaria KLCC** (p34).

Go mall-hopping to **Pavilion KL** (p46), **Starhill Gallery** (p47) and **Lot 10** (p48) along Jln Bukit Bintang until 10pm. If you need it, indulge in a massage at **Donna Spa** (p34). Then head to Changkat Bukit Bintang and Jln Mesui for the bars; **Pisco Bar** (p41) is a good choice. Also check out **No Black Tie** (p43) for its jazz and classical concerts.

Day Two

Admire the historic buildings of **Merdeka Square** (p54) – if you can, sign up for one of Visit KL's free tours – then either cycle on a hired bike or take a taxi to the **Tun Abdul Razak Heritage Park** (p94). Start at the **National Monument** (p105), then walk through the Perdana Botanical Garden** (p95) to the **National Museum** (p102); if you're there by 10am you can take the free guided tour

Continue to enjoy the leafy surrounds of the park at the **KL Bird Park** (p103) or **Butterfly Park** (p103). Save a couple of hours for the splendid **Islamic Arts Museum** (p96), then admire the architecture of **Masjid Negara** (p102) and **old KL train station** (p105).

Go souvenir shopping at the **Central Market** (p61), then push your way through the crowds at Chinatown's **Petaling Street Market** (p70). Finish up with a cocktail at speakeasy-style bars **PS150** (p68) or **Omakase + Appreciate** (p68).

hort on time?

e've arranged Kuala Lumpur's must-sees into these day-by-day itineraries to make
ure you see the very best of the city in the time you have available.

ay Three

☀ Have breakfast at **Bazaar Baru Chow Kit** (p84), one of KL's most tmospheric wet markets, then amble
rough the Malay area of **Kampung aru** (p78) admiring the traditional
ooden houses and flower gardens.

☀ Walk from **Masjid India** (p79) to Bukit Nanas, where you can
raverse the canopy walkway of the **KL orest Eco Park** (p27) and then go much
igher up the **Menara Kuala Lumpur** p26), to get your bearings in the city
rom the observation deck, and, weather ermitting, the new outdoor deck.

🌙 For another panoramic perspective of KL, stand on the upper
erraces of the gloriously decorative
Thean Hou Temple (p115). Walk around
he many religious sites of Brickfields in
the cool of evening and enjoy a cocktail
at the rooftop **Mai Bar** (p110) overlook-
ng KL Sentral.

Day Four

☀ Climb the 272 steps at **Batu Caves** (p88) to pay your respects
at the Hindu **Temple Cave** (p89) and learn about bats and other cave dwellers
in the **Dark Cave** (p89).

☀ View the city skyline from **Titiwangsa Lake Gardens** (p78),
where you can hire a bike, take a boat out on the lake or even go for a spin in a
helicopter. Nearby is the **National Visual Arts Gallery** (p78).

🌙 Sink a sunset cocktail at **Heli Lounge Bar** (p40), then splash
out on dinner at **Antara Restaurant** (p65) at Old Malaya or **Cantaloupe** (p37)
at Troika. If your budget doesn't stretch to fine dining, a meal on **Jalan Alor** (p29)
will be equally memorable and delicious. End the night at the new entertainment
complex TREC by seeing some stand-up comedy or live music at **Live House**
(p127) or clubbing until the early hours at **Zouk** (p127).

Need to Know

For more information,
see Survival Guide (p139)

Currency
Malaysian Ringgit (RM)

Languages
Bahasa Malaysia
English

Visas
Generally not required for stays of up to
60 days.

Money
ATMs widely available; credit cards
accepted in most hotels and restaurants.

Mobile Phones
Local SIM cards can be used in most
phones; if not, set your phone to roaming.

Time
MYT (Malaysia Time; UTC/GMT plus eight
hours)

Tipping
Not generally expected, but leaving small
change in a cafe or restaurant is appreciated.
Many restaurants in KL add a service charge
of around 10% onto the bill.

① Before You Go

Your Daily Budget

Budget: Less than RM100

▶ Dorm bed: RM17–50

▶ Hawker stalls and food courts for meals

▶ Use public transport; plan sightseeing
around walking tours, free museums and
galleries

Midrange: RM100–400

▶ Double room in a comfortable hotel:
RM100–400

▶ Two-course meal in a neighbourhood
restaurant: RM40–60

▶ Take taxis and guided tours

Top end: More than RM400

▶ Luxury double room: RM450–1000

▶ Meal in top restaurant plus bottle of wine:
RM200

Useful Websites

Visit KL (www.visitkl.gov.my) Official city
tourism site.

Time Out KL (www.timeoutkl.com) Monthly
listings magazine with an excellent website.

Lonely Planet (www.lonelyplanet.com/
kuala-lumpur) Destination information, hotel
bookings, traveller forum and more.

Advance Planning

Two months before Book tickets for a concert at the Dewan Filharmonik Petronas.

One month before Plan your itinerary,
checking to see if there are any events or
festivals you may be able to attend.

One week before Book online for a tour up
Petronas Towers and a foodie walking tour.
Make reservations at top-end restaurants.

2 Arriving in Kuala Lumpur

ost likely you'll arrive at Kuala Lumpur ternational Airport (KLIA), although a ndful of flights land at SkyPark Subang rminal. Coming overland, arrival points lude KL Sentral for trains and Terminal rsepadu Selatan (TBS) for buses. Ferries m Sumatra (Indonesia) dock at Pelabuhan ang, which is connected by rail with Sentral.

From Kuala Lumpur ternational Airport (KLIA)

ain RM55; every 15 minutes from 5am to m; 30 minutes to KL Sentral.

us RM10; every hour from 5am to 1am; one ur to KL Sentral.

axi From RM75; one hour to central KL.

From KL Sentral

ansport hub with train, light rail (LRT), onorail, bus and taxi links to rest of city.

Terminal Bersepadu Selatan

ong-distance buses from most destinations ow arrive here. It's connected to KL by LRT.

3 Getting Around

KL Sentral is the hub of a rail-based urban network consisting of the KTM Komuter, KLIA Ekspres, KLIA Transit, light rail (LRT) and monorail systems. Though the systems are poorly integrated, you can happily get around much of central KL on a combination of rail and monorail services. Buy the **MyRapid card** (www.myrapid.com.my; RM10) at mono-rail and LRT stations; it can also be used on Rapid KL buses.

Monorail

Stops in mostly convenient locations; gets very crowded during evening rush hours.

LRT

Handy (for Chinatown, Kampung Baru, KLCC), but network is poorly integrated.

Bus

The GOKL City Bus has four free loop services connecting many city-centre destinations.

Taxi

Can be flagged down with metered fares. At some designated taxi ranks a prepaid coupon system for journeys operates.

Kuala Lumpur Neighbourhoods

Worth a Trip

◉ **Top Sights**

Forestry Research Institute of Malaysia (FRIM; p90)

Batu Caves (p88)

Thean Hou Temple (p114)

Worth a Trip

◯ **Local Life**

Pudu (p50)

Bangsar Baru (p116)

Lake Gardens & Brickfields (p92)

The city's green lungs are surrounded by top museums, while south is KL's official Little India.

◉ **Top Sights**

Tun Abdul Razak Heritage Park

Islamic Arts Museum

◉ **Tun Abdul Razak Heritage Park**

◉ **Merdeka Square**

◉ **Islamic Arts Museum**

◉ **Sri Mahamariamman Temple**

Masjid India & Kampung Baru (p74)
These distinct ethnic neighborhoods attract with lively markets and a *kampung* (village) in the heart of the city.

Bukit Bintang & KLCC (p22)
Here KL shows off with gleaming skyscrapers and chic bars – it's the place to head for malls, street food, restaurants and clubs.

◉ Top Sights

Petronas Towers

Menara Kuala Lumpur

Chinatown & Merdeka Square (p52)
Historical architecture, from Moghul mosques to colonial mansions, and Chinese and Indian cuisine, make this KL's most popular tourist area.

◉ Top Sights

Merdeka Square

Sri Mahamariamman Temple

Menara Kuala Lumpur

◉

Petronas Towers

◉

Explore
Kuala Lumpur

Worth a Trip

Entrance to Batu Caves
R.NAGY / SHUTTERSTOCK ©

Explore

Bukit Bintang & KLCC

Bukit Bintang (Star Hill) – also known as the Golden Triangle – is home to a cluster of major shopping malls and many excellent places to eat and drink, not least of which is Jln Alor, KL's most famous food street. KLCC, which stands for Kuala Lumpur City Centre, is the vast development anchored by the Petronas Towers.

The Sights in a Day

☼ Head to KLCC and start the day with a tour of the **Petronas Towers** (p24). Head to the mall below the towers, **Suria KLCC** (p47), for some shopping before visiting **Galeri Petronas** (p33) – the free art exhibitions are excellent.

☼ Grab lunch at the **Dharma Realm Guan Yin Sagely Monastery** (p36), a favourite with locals. Take a stroll around **KLCC Park** (p25), then head to the **ILHAM** (p32) for a look at its collections of contemporary Malaysian art. Next, choose between learning about sealife at **Aquaria KLCC** (p34) or taking a 3pm tour of the Malay-style stilt house **Rumah Penghulu Abu Seman** (p33).

☾ After dinner at **Bijan** (p36), take advantage of the evening opening hours of some of KL's many malls. Try **Pavilion KL** (p46), **Starhill Gallery** (p47) and **Lot 10** (p29). End the evening with drinks on Jln Mesui; try a pisco sour at **Pisco Bar** (p41) or check out some live music at **No Black Tie** (p43).

For a local's day in Bukit Bintang, see p28.

👁 Top Sights

🔍 Local Life

♥ Best of Kuala Lumpur

Getting There

 Monorail The best way to access the area with stops along Jln Imbi and Jln Sultan Ismail. Avoid the evening weekday rush hour, from 6pm to 8pm.

🚌 **Bus** There are four free GOKL City Bus loop services, but they can get snarled in traffic.

🚈 **MRT** New stations Bukit Bintang and Tun Razak Exchange due to open in 2017.

Top Sights
Petronas Towers

Resembling two silver rockets preparing for take-off, the twin towers of Kuala Lumpur's iconic landmark are the perfect allegory for the meteoric rise of the city from tin-miners' hovel to 21st-century metropolis. The magnificent stainless steel skyscrapers are the crowning glory of KLCC.

Twin Towers

Opened in 1998, the Petronas Towers reach up nearly 452m; for six years they were the tallest structure in the world and they remain the

Map p30, D2

☏ 03-2331 8080

www.petronastwintowers.
com.my

Jln Ampang

adult/child RM85/35

⊘ 9am-9pm Tue-Sun, closed
1-2.30pm Fri

🚇 KLCC

world's tallest twin towers. The design for the 88-storey-high tower blocks, by Argentinian architect César Pelli, is based on an eight-sided star that echoes arabesque patterns. Islamic influences are also evident in each tower's five tiers – representing the five pillars of Islam – and in the 63m masts that crown them, calling to mind the minarets of a mosque and the Star of Islam.

The starting point for guided 45-minute tours of the towers is the ticket office in the towers' basement. First stop is the **Skybridge** connection on the 41st floors of the towers at 170m. Having walked across this you'll then take the lift up to the 86th-floor **observation deck** at 370m.

Concert Hall

Tucked away at the base of the Petronas Towers is KLCC's premier concert hall, Dewan Filharmonik Petronas (p44), a handsomely decorated space with excellent acoustics. The polished Malaysian Philharmonic Orchestra (www.mpo.com.my) plays here (usually Friday and Saturday evening and Sunday matinee, but also other times) as well as other local and international ensembles.

KLCC Park

The Petronas Towers are the star attraction of KLCC (Kuala Lumpur City Centre), a development covering 40 hectares of land that was once the Selangor Turf Club. The site includes the imaginatively landscaped **KLCC Park** (⏾7am-10pm), designed by Brazilian Roberto Burle Marx, who never lived to see its completion. Naturally, the park is the best vantage point for photos of the Petronas Towers. In the early evening, it can seem like everyone in town has come down here to watch the glowing towers punching up into the night sky.

☑ Top Tips

▶ Buy your ticket online. Up to half of the 1500 tickets issued daily can be bought via the website until 24 hours before the visit time.

▶ If you don't have an advance booking, get in line around 8.30am to be sure of securing one of the remaining tickets.

▶ Go early for the best views. Mornings in KL tend to be clearer than afternoons, when it is more likely to rain or be hazy.

✕ Take a Break

For a lip-smackingly good bowl of noodles head to Little Penang Kafé (p37), one of tens of dining options at Suria KLCC, the mall adjacent to the towers.

Across the road at Avenue K is the family-friendly restaurant **Wondermama** (www.wondermama.my; ground flr, Ave K, 156 Jln Ampang; mains RM13-27; ⏾10am-9.30pm; ♿; 🚇KLCC) selling tasty modern Malaysian food.

Top Sights
Menara Kuala Lumpur

Located within the KL Forest Eco Park, this 421m telecommunications tower, the tallest in Southeast Asia and seventh-tallest in the world, offers the city's best views. Come to appreciate the phenomenal growth of the city while enjoying a Malay banquet or afternoon tea at the tower's sky-high revolving restaurant, or to explore the park's treetops on the canopy walkway.

Map p30, B3

www.menarakl.com.my

2 Jln Punchak

observation deck adult/child RM52/31, open deck adults only RM105

⊘ observation deck 9am-10pm, last tickets 9.30pm

🚊 KL Tower

View of Menara Kuala Lumpur

Observation Decks

Although the Petronas Towers are taller structures, the Menara KL (KL Tower) provides a higher viewpoint as its base is already nearly 100m above sea level atop Bukit Nanas. A lift whisks you up 276m to the indoor observation deck in the bulb at the top of the tower, its shape inspired by a Malaysian spinning toy. More thrilling yet is the **open air deck** at 300m, access to which is weather dependent. Here you can take photos unencumbered by windows and step (if you dare) into the new **sky box** jutting out from the deck which puts nothing but glass between you and the ground below.

KL Forest Eco Park

The best way to approach the tower is via the 200m-long canopy walkway which climbs up through the **KL Forest Eco Park** (Taman Eko Rimba KL; ☎03-2026 4741; www.forestry.gov.my; admission free; ☻7am-6pm) in nine sections, beginning just behind the **Forest Information Centre** (☎03-2026 4741; www.forestry.gov.my; Jln Raja Chulan; admission free; ☻9am-5pm) on Jln Raja Chulan. Known until recently as the Bukit Nanas Forest Reserve, this lowland dipterocarp forest reserve covering 9.37 hectares was gazetted in 1906 making it the oldest protected piece of jungle in Malaysia. The park also has several short, interconnected trails and an impressive bamboo walk that are worth exploring. The entrance to the trails is signposted near the top of the canopy walkway, but pick up a map at the information centre and ask which trails are open before setting out.

Other attractions

There's plenty of touristy hoopla at the tower base including a zoo, an F1 simulator and a small aquarium. Look out too for the 150-year-old **Jelutong tree** that was saved during the tower's construction – find it to the left of the tower lobby.

☑ **Top Tips**

▶ Start at the KL Forest Eco Park information centre on Jln Raja Chulan and walk up to the tower through the forest via the canopy walkway.

▶ The open deck tickets include access to the sky box.

✕ **Take a Break**

Make a reservation for a buffet lunch, dinner or afternoon tea at tower-top restaurant **Atmosphere 360** (☎03-2020 2121; www.atmosphere360.com.my; buffet lunch/afternoon tea/dinner RM92/60/208; ☻11.30am-1pm, 3.30-5.30pm & 6.30-11pm), where the food comes with views.

At ground level, stop for tasty Punjabi food at **Moghul Mahal** (☎03-2070 8288; www.moghul-mahal.com.my; mains RM20-48; ☻10am-11pm).

Local Life
A Taste of Bukit Bintang

Street food is everywhere in Bukit Bintang, though in KL locals accept it neither has to be prepared nor consumed outdoors. Given the city's obsession with malls and air-conditioning, many hawker stalls have moved indoors, though if you want it old-school this area still shines.

❶ Restoran Win Heng Seng

Often hawkers congregate in a single streetside food court such as at **Restoran Win Heng Seng** (183 Jln Imbi; dishes RM5-10; ⏰6.30am-midnight; AirAsia-Bukit Bintang), a popular place for a local breakfast. Try the pork ball noodles or the *char kway teow* (fried noodles in a dark soy sauce).

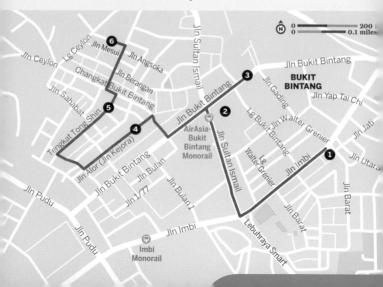

❷ Lot 10 Hutong

The first KL mall to encourage top hawkers to open branches in a basement food court, **Lot 10 Hutong** (basement, lot 10, 50 Jln Sultan Ismail; dishes RM9-18; ☺10am-10pm; 🚊AirAsia-Bukit Bintang) is a well-designed space. It has pulled in names such as Soong Kee, which has served beef noodles since 1945. Look also for oyster omelettes at Kong Tai, Cantonese porridge at Hon Kee, and Hokkien mee at Kim Lian Kee.

❸ Bintang Walk

This short strip of prime real estate is tops for people-watching. **Al-Amar Express** (📞03-2141 3814; www.al-amar.com; 179 Jln Bukit Bintang; mains RM11-23; ☺10am-midnight; 🚊AirAsia-Bukit Bintang), a glass-encased streetside restaurant, is a great place to take it all in with a Turkish coffee.

❹ Jalan Alor

KL's biggest collection of roadside restaurants sprawls along **Jalan Alor** (🚊AirAsia-Bukit Bintang). From around 5pm till late every evening, the street transforms into a continuous open-air venue. Most places serve alcohol and you can sample pretty much every Malay-Chinese dish imaginable. In the afternoon you can pick up a fortifying fresh coconut or sugarcane drink and watch the preparation for the nightly feast.

❺ Tengkat Tong Shin

Here's another short street loaded with restaurants and hawker stalls. Among the most celebrated is the nothing-to-look-at **Ngau Kee** (Tengkat Tong Shin; noodles RM8-9; ☺6pm-4am; AirAsia-Bukit Bintang) at the end of the street, which serves a variety of beef noodle soups. Don't miss **Tong Shin Hokkien Mee** (Tengkat Tong Shin, near cnr Jln Tong Shin; mains RM7; ☺7.30pm-midnight Wed-Mon; 🚊AirAsia-Bukit Bintang), prepared in the traditional style with pork lard, soy sauce, lardons and prawns and cooked over a charcoal flame to add a smokey flavour. It's a popular place, but once you tuck in you'll be glad you waited. If you aren't hungry, Tengkat Tong Shin's art deco and eclectic-style pre-war shophouses are worth a look-in.

❻ Changkat Bukit Bintang & Jalan Mesui

The last two blocks of Changkat Bukit Bintang support a number of bars that offer everything from a lounge for contemplating single malt whisky to a corner den for cheap draught and pub quizzes. Around the corner, on Jln Mesui, head to No Black Tie (p43) for live jazz and classical music.

E F G H

Mayang

25
Jln Tun Razak

Ampamg
Park
LRT

Jln Ampang

1

KLCC
LRT

10

36

Dharma Realm
Guan Yin Sagely
Monastery

13 ILHAM
1

Tabung
Haji

Jln Ampang

33

85

Galeri
Petronas

Persiaran KLCC

Jln Birjai

2

trosains

Kuala Lumpur
City Centre
(KLCC)
Park

Jln Tun Razak

3

Aquaria
5 KLCC

Jln Stonor

Pinang Jln Kia Peng

Persiaran Stonor

Jln Stonor

Jln Kia Peng

4

Rumah
Penghulu
Abu Seman

Jln Conlay

Jln Tun Razak

3

Jln Conlay

Muzium
6 Kraf

32

Jln Raja Chulan

Jln Bukit Bintang

Jln Bukit Bintang

5

8 Donna Spa

Jln Imbi

7 Starhill Culinary

Jln Gading

Studio

31

34

Spa
2 Village

Sights

ILHAM

GALLERY

1 ⊙ Map p30, G1

KL's latest public art gallery provides an excellent reason to admire close-up the slick 60-storey ILHAM Tower designed by Foster + Partners. With a mission to showcase modern and contemporary Malaysian art, ILHAM kicked off with a blockbuster show of works by Hoessein Enas (1924–95). There's no permanent collection, with exhibitions changing every three to four months. (www.ilhamgallery.com; 3rd & 5th fl, Ilham Tower, 8 Jln Binjai; admission free; ⊙11am-7pm Tue-Sat, to 5pm Sun; 🚇Ampang Park)

Spa Village

SPA

2 ⊙ Map p30, F5

A beautifully landscaped pool with waterfalls and greenery creates a tranquil setting for this first-rate spa. Signature treatments include the traditional Royal Malay couples spa experience (including a massage, scrub, scented body steaming and shared herbal bath in a private garden area) and a Chinese Peranakan treatment involving a rattan tapping massage, and pearl and rice facial. (☎03-2782 9090; www.spavillage.com; Ritz-Carlton, 168 Jln Imbi; treatments RM410-995; ⊙10am-10pm; 🚇AirAsia-Bukit Bintang)

Understand

Visual Arts in Kuala Lumpur

Malaysia has an impressive contemporary-art scene and KL is the best place to access it, both at public galleries and in several private collections that are open to visitors by appointment.

Among the most interesting and internationally successful contemporary Malaysian artists are Jalaini Abu Hassan ('Jai'), Wong Hoy Cheong, landscape painter Wong Perng Fey and Australian-trained multimedia artist Yee I-Lann. Amron Omar has focused for nearly 30 years on *silat* (a Malay martial art) as a source of inspiration for his paintings, a couple of which hang in the National Visual Arts Gallery in KL.

Latiff Mohidin, who is also a poet, is a Penang-based artist whose work spans several decades and has featured in a major retrospective at the National Visual Arts Gallery; he's considered a national treasure.

Abdul Multhalib Musa's sculptures have won awards; he created several pieces in Beijing for the 2008 Olympics. One of Musa's rippling steel-tube creations can be spotted outside Wisma Selangor Dredging, 142C Jln Ampang, in KL.

Blueface angelfish, Aquaria KLCC (p34)

Rumah Penghulu Abu Seman
HISTORIC BUILDING

3 ⊙ Map p30, F4

This glorious wooden stilt house, which was once the family home of a village headman in Kedah, was built in stages between 1910 and the 1930s and later moved to the grounds of **Badan Warisan Malaysia** (Heritage of Malaysia Trust; ☎03 2144 9273; www.badan-warisan.org.my; admission free; ◷10am-4pm Tue-Sat; ⬚Raja Chulan). Worthwhile tours of the property provide an explanation of the house's architecture and history and of Malay customs and traditional village life. You can wander around outside tour times (and since it's built with ventilation in mind, you can easily look in). (2 Jln Stonor; suggested donation RM10; ◷tours 11am & 3pm Mon-Sat; ⬚Raja Chulan)

Galeri Petronas
GALLERY

4 ⊙ Map p30, E2

Swap consumerism for culture at this excellent art gallery showcasing contemporary photography and paintings. It's a bright, modern space with interesting, professionally curated shows that change every few months. (☎03-2051 7770; www.galeripetronas.com.my; 3rd fl, Suria KLCC, Jln Ampang; admission free; ◷10am-8pm Tue-Sun; ⬚KLCC)

Top Tip
Menara vs Petronas

The choice between a trip up the Menara KL or Petronas Towers is a tricky one. Both offer stupendous views over the city, but if you want to see KL on a whim, or have forgotten to book ahead, then Menara KL is the better choice. There are rarely queues, even on weekends, and you can be up and down in 30 minutes and follow it with a walk through the jungle down to Chinatown.

Aquaria KLCC   AQUARIUM

 5 ◉ Map p30, E3

The highlight of this impressive aquarium in the basement of the KL Convention Centre is its 90m underwater tunnel: view sand tiger sharks, giant gropers and more up close. Daily feeding sessions for a variety of fish and otters are complemented by ones for arapaimas, electric eels and sharks on Monday, Wednesday and Saturday (see website for schedule). Free dives (RM424), cage dives (RM211), and a Sleep with Sharks (RM211) program for kids aged six to 13 are also available. (☑03-2333 1888; www.aquariaklcc.com; Concourse, KL Convention Centre, Jln Pinang; adult/child RM64/53; ⊙10am-8pm, last admission 7pm; ⛫; ⧉KLCC)

Muzium Kraf   MUSEUM

 6 ◉ Map p30, G4

At the back of the **Kompleks Kraf shop** (☑03-2162 7533; www.kraftangan.gov.my/en/craft-complex-2; ⊙9am-8pm) is this sur-

prisingly good museum dedicated to Malaysia's traditional crafts. There are special exhibits and regular displays of batik, wood carving, pewter, kites and drums. Exhibits are nicely accompanied by informative posters. (☑03-2162 7459; www.muzium-kraf.blogspot.co.uk; Jln Conlay; adult/child RM3/1; ⊙9am-5pm; Raja Chulan)

Starhill Culinary Studio   COOKING

 7 ◉ Map p30, E5

Sign up for a two- to three-hour class (usually focusing on a single dish) and you'll not only get top instruction in this gleaming, well-designed culinary art studio, but you'll also be well fed. Classes vary daily and include Malay and Nonya (Peranakan) dishes, Japanese cuisine, baking and Asian and Western desserts. Private classes can also be arranged. (☑03-2782 3810; www.starhillculinarystudio.com; Starhill Gallery, Muse Fl, 181 Jln Bukit Bintang; public classes RM188; ⊙10am-9.30pm Tue-Sun; ⧉AirAsia-Bukit Bintang)

Donna Spa   SPA

8 ◉ Map p30, E5

This Balinese-style spa is one of the most popular on the well-named Pamper Floor of the slick Starhill Gallery mall (p47). One-hour massages start at RM260, and full spa packages including wraps and scrubs at RM490. (☑03-2141 8999; www.donnaspa.net; Pamper Fl, Starhill Gallery, 181 Jln Bukit Bintang; ⊙10am-midnight; ⧉AirAsia-Bukit Bintang)

Understand

Multiculturalism, Religion & Culture

Since the interracial riots of 1969, when distrust between the Malays and Chinese peaked, Malaysia has forged a more tolerant multicultural society. The emergence of a single 'Malaysian' identity is now a much-discussed concept, even if it is far from being actually realised. Religious and ethnic tensions are a fact of life in KL, where the different communities coexist rather than mingle.

The Malays

All Malays, Muslims by birth, are supposed to follow Islam, but many also adhere to older spiritual beliefs and adat. With its roots in the Hindu period, adat places great emphasis on collective responsibility and maintaining harmony within the community.

The enduring appeal of the communal *kampung* (village) spirit shouldn't be underestimated – many an urban Malay hankers after it, despite the affluent Western-style living conditions they enjoy at home.

The Chinese

Religious customs govern much of the Chinese community's home life, from the moment of birth, which is carefully recorded for astrological consultations later in life, to funerals, which also have many rites and rituals. There's also a strong attachment to the original area of China from where a family originated, seen in the attachment of families to specific temples or *kongsi* (clan houses).

If there's one cultural aspect that all Malaysian Chinese agree on it's the importance of education. It has been a very sensitive subject among the Malaysian Chinese community since the introduction in the early 1970s of government policies that favour Malays.

The Indians

Indians in Malaysia hail from many parts of the subcontinent and have different cultures depending on their religions – mainly Hinduism, Islam, Sikhism and Christianity. Most are Tamils, originally coming from the area now known as Tamil Nadu in southern India, where Hindu traditions are strong. Later, Muslim Indians from northern India followed, along with Sikhs.

Local Life
Food Courts

KLites know that food courts are the best place to refuel during a hard day's shopping at the malls. You'll be spoilt for choice at the Pavilion food court **Food Republic** (☑03-2142 8006; www.foodrepublic. com.my; level 1, Pavilion KL, 168 Jln Bukit Bintang; mains RM5-17; ⏰10am-10pm; AirAsia-Bukit Bintang), or sample the wares of some of the city's top hawkers at the stalls at the food court Lot 10 Hutong (p29).

Petrosains   MUSEUM

9 Map p30, E2

Fill an educational few hours at this interactive science discovery centre with all sorts of buttons to press and levers to pull. Many of the activities and displays focus on the wonderful things that fuel has brought to Malaysia – no prizes for guessing who sponsors the museum. As a side note, 'sains' is not pronounced 'sayns' but 'science'. (☑03-2331 8181; www.petrosains. com.my; 4th fl, Suria KLCC, Jln Ampang; adult/child RM30/18; ⏰9.30am-4pm Tue-Fri, to 5pm Sat & Sun; ⓘ; KLCC)

Dharma Realm Guan Yin Sagely Monastery   BUDDHIST TEMPLE

10 Map p30, F1

The calm spaces, potted plants, mandala ceilings and giant gilded statues create an appropriately contemplative mood for quiet meditation at this col-ourful modern temple. The complex is dedicated to Guan Yin, the Buddhist goddess of compassion, represented by the central statue in the main building. There's an excellent vegan **canteen** (mains RM6-10; ⏰11am-2.30pm Mon-Fri; ✈) behind the complex staffed by volunteers and monks. (www.drba. org; 161 Jln Ampang; admission free; ⏰7am-4pm; Ampang Park)

Eating

Bijan   MALAYSIAN $$$

11 Map p30, C5

One of KL's best Malaysian restaurants, Bijan offers skilfully cooked traditional dishes in a sophisticated dining room that spills out into a tropical garden. Must-try dishes include *rendang daging* (dry beef curry with lemongrass), *masak lemak ikan* (Penang-style fish curry with turmeric) and *ikan panggang* (grilled skate with tamarind). (☑03-2031 3575; www.bijanrestaurant.com; 3 Jln Ceylon; mains RM30-90; ⏰4.30-11pm; Raja Chulan)

Sushi Hinata   JAPANESE $$$

12 Map p30, C4

It's quite acceptable to use your fingers to savour the sublime sushi served at the counter, one piece at a time, by expert Japanese chefs from Nagoya. There are also private booths for more intimate dinners. The kaiseki-style full course meals are edible works of art. (☑03-2022 1349;

www.shin-hinata.com; Gt Mary Residence, Jln Tengah; lunch/dinner set meals from RM77/154; ⊘noon-3pm & 6-11pm Mon-Sat; Raja Chulan)

Little Penang Kafé MALAYSIAN $$

At peak meal times expect a long line outside this mall joint (see **35** Map p30, E2) serving authentic food from Penang, including specialities such as curry mee (spicy soup noodles with prawns). (☑03-2163 0215; level 4, Suria KLCC, Jln Ampang; mains RM14-22; ⊘11.30am-9.30pm; 🚇KLCC)

Ben's INTERNATIONAL $$

The flagship brand of the BIG group of dining outlets (see **32** Map p30, E5) delivers on both style and substance. There's a tempting range of Eastern and Western comfort foods, appealing living-room design and nice touches such as a box of cards with recipes and talk topics on each table. Other branches are in Suria KLCC, Publika and Bangsar Shopping Centre. (☑03-2141 5290; www.thebiggroup.co/bens; level 6, Pavilion KL, 168 Jln Bukit Bintang; mains RM25-78; ⊘11am-11pm; 🛜; 🚇AirAsia-Bukit Bintang)

Cantaloupe FRENCH $$$

13 Map p30, G1

The French fine-dining section of Troika Sky Dining is an elegant space (but watch you don't step in the floor-level water feature; we're told 48 people ended up with wet feet last year). A set lunch allows a sampling

of their fancy style (think sea urchin with almond custard and yuzu foam) but is unlikely to fill you up. (☑03-2162 0886; www.troikaskydining.com; level 23a, tower B, The Troika, Persiaran KLCC; set lunches RM120, 4-/6-/8-course dinners RM250/360/450; ⊘noon-2pm Mon-Fri, 6.30-10.30pm daily; 🚇Ampang Park)

Rococo CAFE $$

14 ❌ Map p30, C5

This atmospheric cafe with views across the rooftops of Jln Alor and Tengkat Tong Shin has a tempting central display of freshly baked bread and homemade pastries, cookies and cakes. Also serves brunch from 11am to 3pm and an all-day menu of salads, sandwiches, pasta and rice dishes. Opens for dinner from 6pm to 10.30pm by reservation only. (☑012-974 0192; www.facebook.com/RococoCafeMY;

✅ Top Tip

Japanese Food

There are tens of thousands of Japanese people living in KL and quality Japanese food is readily available. At Pavilion KL mall's Tokyo Street, slurp tasty ramen noodles at **Santouka** (☑03-2143 8878; www.santouka.co.jp/en; level 6, Pavilion KL, 168 Jln Bukit Bintang; ramen sets RM30-40; ⊘11am-10pm; 🚇AirAsia-Bukit Bintang), a branch of the famous stall from the island of Hokkaido.

Curry laksa

7th fl, Melange Boutique Hotel, 14 Jln Rembia; mains RM14-30; ⏱11am-10.30pm Wed-Mon; AirAsia-Bukit Bintang)

Melur & Thyme   FUSION $$

This appealingly designed restaurant's name, conjoining Malay and Western ingredients, hints at its game plan: offering Malay and Western tapas-sized portions to be mixed and shared (see **35** 🔒 Map p30, E2). For breakfast (8am to 11am) the coconut pancakes with caramelised honeydew melon is a very tasty precursor to a day's shopping in Suria KLCC. (✆03-2181 8001; www.melurandthyme.com; ground fl, Suria KLCC, Jln Ampang; mains RM14-59; ⏱8am-9.30pm; 🚆KLCC)

Pinchos Tapas Bar   TAPAS $$

15 🍴 Map p30, A1

This is the real deal for tapas, run by a Spaniard and packed with KL's approving Spanish-speaking community. A great place for a solo meal and drink or fun with a group while you munch your way through the wide-ranging menu. (✆03-2145 8482; www.pinchos.com.my; 18 Changat Bukit Bintang; tapas RM18-66; ⏱food 5-11pm, bar to 3am, Tue-Sun; 🚆Raja Chulan)

Lima Blas   PERANAKAN $$

16 🍴 Map p30, A1

With a hip, bric-a-brac design that channels old Malaysia to a T, this restaurant and open-air bar is a top

Understand

Kuala Lumpur's Cuisine

KL is a nonstop feast. You can dine in incredible elegance or mingle with locals at street stalls, taking your pick from a global array of cuisines. Ingredients are fresh, the cooking is high quality, hygiene standards are excellent and the final bill is seldom heavy on the pocket.

Chinese

Thanks to generations of immigrants from all parts of China, KL boasts a notable range of regional Chinese cuisines. The city is famous for chilli *pan mee,* wheat noodles tossed with dark soy sauce and garlic oil, garnished with chopped pork and crispy *ikan bilis* (dried sardines or anchovies), and served with soup on the side. Hainanese immigrants were the private cooks of the British during colonial rule, which has led to a hybrid style of Western cuisine still served in old-school eateries, such as Yut Kee (p83).

Malay & Peranakan

Head to Kampung Baru to sample the specialities of Malaysia's eastern states, such as Kelantanese *nasi kerabu* (blue rice) and *ayam percik* (barbecued chicken smothered in chilli-coconut sauce) and, from Terengganu, *nasi dagang* (nutty, coconut-milk-cooked red rice). Also look out across the city for restaurants serving Peranakan (or Nonya) cuisine, a fusion of Chinese and Malay ingredients and cooking techniques.

Indian

KL's two Little Indias – the official one in Brickfields and the other around Masjid India – are the places to sample Indian cooking, although you'll find the cuisine of the subcontinent served across the city. A very KL experience is eating late at night at an Indian Muslim eatery known as a *mamak;* these typically run 24 hours, serve comfort-food dishes such as *roti canai* (flaky flatbread), mee goreng (fried noodles) and *murtabak* (pancakes stuffed with meat).

Local Life
Jalan Alor Street Eats

The restaurants on Jln Alor serve a variety of Malay, Chinese and Southeast Asian staples. Try **Wong Ah Wah** (WAW; 1-9 Jln Alor; chicken wings per piece RM3.20; ⏱5pm-4am; 🚇AirAsia-Bukit Bintang), justly famous for its seriously addictive chicken wings; **Sisters Noodle** (21a Jln Alor; noodles RM6; ⏱7am-4pm; 🚇AirAsia-Bukit Bintang) for delicious 'drunken' chicken mee (noodles) made with rice wine; or go for fiery Sichuan at **Kedai Makanan Dan Minuman TKS** (32 Jln Alor; small mains RM15-35; ⏱6pm-4am; 🚇AirAsia-Bukit Bintang).

spot for a casual night out of exotic food and postdinner drinks. Try the Nonya fried chicken, aubergine in sambal sauce and the *sago gula melaka* (sago pearls in a brown-sugar sauce). (📞03-2110 1681; www.facebook.com/limablas25; 25 Jln Mesui; mains RM19-33; ⏱kitchen 11am-3pm & 6-10.30pm Mon-Sat, bar to midnight Mon-Thu, to 1am Fri & Sat; 🛜; 🚇Raja Chulan)

Sao Nam　　　VIETNAMESE $$

17 Map p30, C5

This reliable place is decorated with colourful communist propaganda posters and has a courtyard for dining outside. The kitchen turns out huge plates of delicious Vietnamese food, garnished with basil, mint, lettuce and sweet dips. The starter *banh xeo* (a huge Vietnamese pancake with meat, seafood or vegetables) is a meal in itself. (📞03-2144 1225; www.saonam.com.my; 25 Tengkat Tong Shin; mains RM30-70; ⏱noon-2.30pm & 7.30-10.30pm Tue-Sun; 🚇AirAsia-Bukit Bintang)

Drinking

Heli Lounge Bar　　　COCKTAIL BAR

18 🍸 Map p30, D4

If the weather's behaving, this is easily the best place for sundowners in KL. Nothing besides your lychee martini and the cocktail waiter stands between you, the edge of the helipad and amazing 360-degree views. Steady your hands as you have to buy your first drink at the somewhat cheesy bar below and carry it up yourself. (📞03-2110 5034; www.facebook.com/Heliloungebar; level 34, Menara KH, Jln Sultan Ishmail; ⏱5pm-midnight Mon-Wed, to 2am Thu, to 3am Fri & Sat, to 11am Sun; 🛜; 🚇Raja Chulan)

Fuego　　　BAR

Part of the Troika complex, Fuego (see 13 ❌ Map p30, G1) shares the same sophisticated ambience and jaw-dropping views as the fine-dining restaurants. The bar has a Latin feel. (📞03-2162 0886; www.troikaskydining.com; level 23a, Tower B, The Troika, Persiaran KLCC; ⏱6pm-midnight; 🚇Ampang Park)

Marini's on 57 BAR

19 Map p30, D2

This is about as close as you can get to eyeballing the upper levels of the Petronas Towers from a bar. The stellar views are complemented by sleek interior design and attentive service. When booking (advised) be aware that it's the lively bar not the laid-back whisky lounge that has the view of the towers. There's also a dress code. (☏03-2386 6030; www.marinis57.com; level 57, Menara 3, Petronas KLCC; ☺5pm-1.30am Sun-Thu, to 3am Fri & Sat; ⍰KLCC)

Feeka Coffee Roasters CAFE

20 Map p30, B1

Set in a minimally remodelled shophouse on hip Jln Mesui, Feeka delivers both on its premium coffee (choose from microlot beans or espresso-based drinks) and its food (breakfast items served from 10am to 6pm and a menu including omelettes and pulled-pork sandwiches served from noon to 10pm, as well as delicious cakes). (www.facebook.com/feeka.coffeeroasters; 19 Jln Mesui; ☺9am 10.30pm Mon-Thu, to 11.30pm Fri-Sun; 🛜; ⍰Raja Chulan)

Neo Tamarind BAR

21 Map p30, C3

This sophisticated restaurant-bar feels like a slice of Bali smuggled into the heart of KL. Sip cocktails by flickering lights and a waterfall running the length of the long bar. The Thai and

Dinosaur display, Petrosains (p36)

Indochinese food is also lovely, should you want to start with dinner. (☏03-2148 3700; www.tamarindrestaurants.com; 19 Jln Sultan Ismail; ☺6-11pm; ⍰Raja Chulan)

Pisco Bar BAR

22 Map p30, B1

Take your pisco sour in the cosy, exposed-brick interior or the plant-filled courtyard of this slick tapas joint. The chef is half Peruvian, so naturally the ceviche here is good. DJs regularly spin the decks at the upstairs dance space on Friday and Saturday nights. (☏03-2142 2900; www.piscobarkl.com; 29 Jln Mesui; ☺5pm-1am Tue, Thu & Sun, to 2am Wed, to 3am Fri & Sat; ⍰Raja Chulan)

Nagaba   BAR

23 🚇 Map p30, B1

This three-level bar and club has a ground-floor industrial-style bar with comfy chairs, and a club on the next floor up. The Rooftop Mojito Bar, with fairy lights, big shared tables and benches, has a DJ deck, has a relaxed, urban vibe. Come from 8pm to 10pm for the all-you-can-drink mojito buffet, with free-flowing cocktails for RM60 per person. (📱03-2141 0858; www.facebook.com/nagaba.kualalumpur; 31 Jln Mesui; ⏰4pm-1am Mon & Tue, to 2am Wed & Thu, to 3am Fri & Sat; 🚇Raja Chulan)

TWG Tea   TEAHOUSE

Offering a mind-boggling range of more than 400 teas and infusions, this KL offshoot of the original Singaporean TWG (see **32** 🔒 Map p30, E5) is a luxurious place to refresh during your rounds of the mall. The teas are beautifully packaged for gifts, too. As well as afternoon tea (2pm to 6pm), it also serves brunch from 10am to 3pm and meals from noon to 10pm. (www.twgtea.com; level 2, Pavilion KL, 168 Jln Bukit Bintang; ⏰10am-10pm; 🚇AirAsia-Bukit Bintang)

Taps Beer Bar   MICROBREWERY

24 🚇 Map p30, D4

Taps specialises in ale from around the world with some 80 different microbrews on rotation, 14 of them on tap. There's live music Thursday to Saturday at 9.30pm and regular beer festivals and events. Taps also serves pub grub (mains RM15 to RM50) and a Sunday roast (RM35 to RM38). (www.tapsbeerbar.my; One Residency, 1 Jln Nagasari; ⏰5pm-1am Mon-Sat, noon-1am Sun; 📶; 🚇Raja Chulan)

Tate   COCKTAIL BAR

25 🚇 Map p30, G1

It's bordering on self-mockery to have a 'secret' speakeasy cocktail bar in a shopping mall, but once you get past that, Tate's sophisticated atmosphere, complete with cushy leather armchairs and a great cocktail menu, is perfect for a relaxing late-night drink. (📱03-2161 2368; www.thebiggroup.co/tate; ground fl, Intermark, 182 Jln Tun Razak; ⏰5pm-2am Mon-Sat; 📶; 🚇Ampang Park)

Q Local Life
RGB at the Bean Hive

This is what you get when a boutique coffee roaster teams with health-conscious cooks in a quiet green oasis. RGB (📱03-2181 1329; www.rathergoodbeans.com; 35 Jln Damai; ⏰9am-4pm Mon, 8.30am-4pm Tue-Fri, 9am-6.30pm Sat & Sun; 📶; 🚇Ampang Park) serves excellent hand-drip coffees and espresso-based drinks as well as vegan and vegetarian breakfasts, sandwiches and pastas, all in a cute bungalow with an inner courtyard and big grassy yard.

Jalan Alor (p40)

Zion Club
CLUB

26 Map p30, A2

This slick new club smack in the middle of the Changkat Bukit Bintang strip has three separate spaces where DJs pump out dance and house, hip-hop and reggae until 5am. There's a happy hour in the reggae bar from 5pm until the club opens at 10pm, after which drink prices skyrocket and a RM50 cover charge applies. (www.facebook.com/theZionKL; 31 Changkat Bukit Bintang; cover charge RM50; 5pm-3am Sun-Tue, to 5am Wed-Sat; AirAsia-Bukit Bintang)

Entertainment

No Black Tie
LIVE MUSIC

27 Map p30, A1

Blink and you'd miss this small live-music venue, bar and bistro as it's hidden behind a grove of bamboo. NBT, as it's known to its faithful patrons, is owned by Malaysian concert pianist Evelyn Hii, who has a knack for finding the talented singer-songwriters, jazz bands and classical-music ensembles who play here from around 9pm. (03-2142 3737; www.noblacktie.com.my; 17 Jln Mesui; live music RM30-70; 5pm-1am Mon-Sat; Raja Chulan)

Dewan Filharmonik Petronas

CONCERT VENUE

28 ⭐ Map p30, D2

Don't miss the chance to attend a show at this gorgeous concert hall at the base of the Petronas Towers (p24). The polished Malaysian Philharmonic Orchestra plays here (usually Friday and Saturday evenings and Sunday matinees, but also other times), as do other local and international ensembles. There is a smart-casual dress code. (📞03-2051 7007; www.dfp. com.my; box office, Tower 2, Petronas Towers, KLCC; ⊗box office 10.30am-6.30pm Tue-Sat; 🚇KLCC)

Forbidden City

LIVE MUSIC

29 ⭐ Map p30, A2

This new live-music venue on Chang-kat Bukit Bintang hosts jazz and blues musicians in a classy, intimate setting. (📞03-2110 2088; www.forbiddencitykl.com; 50a Changkat Bukit Bintang; ⊗9pm-1am Tue-Thu, to 2am Fri & Sat; 🚇AirAsia-Bukit Bintang)

KL Live

LIVE MUSIC

30 ⭐ Map p30, C3

A boon to KL's live-music scene, this spacious venue packs in rock and pop fans with an impressive lineup of over-seas and local big-name artists and DJs. (📞03-2162 2570; www.kl-live.com.my; 1st fl, Life Centre, 20 Jln Sultan Ismail; Raja Chulan)

Understand
Gay & Lesbian Kuala Lumpur

Malaysia is a predominantly Muslim country and the level of tolerance for homosexuality is vastly different from those of its neighbours. Sex between men is illegal and sharia Islamic laws also forbid cross-dressing. Outright persecution of gays and lesbians is rare. Nonetheless, LGBT travellers should avoid behaviour that may attract unwanted attention; Malaysians are con-servative about displays of public affection regardless of sexual orientation.

That said, there's a fairly open gay scene in KL, with several established gay dance nights, the main ones being **DivineBliss** (G Tower Rooftop; www. facebook.com/Divine.KL; rooftop, G Tower, 199 Jln Tun Razak; RM45; ⊗10pm-3am Sat; 🚇Ampang Park) at G Tower and Lovemachine at **Marketplace** (📞03-2166 0750; www.facebook.com/love.mpkl; 4a Lg Yap Kwan Seng; RM40; ⊗10pm-3am Fri & Sat; 🚇KLCC). Also don't miss the monthly party **Rainbow Rojak** (www.facebook. com/RainbowRojak); this laid-back and inclusive event for all sexual persua-sions is currently held at Marketplace. The lesbian scene is more discreet, but it exists for those willing to seek it out. Start looking for information on www.utopia-asia.com or www.fridae.com.

KLCC Park (p25)

GSC Pavilion KL   CINEMA

Expect queues for hit movies at this multiplex in the popular Pavilion mall (see **32** 🅰 Map p30, E5). This is one of the few multiplexes in the GSC chain that has an International Screens program showing art-house and foreign movies. (www.gsc.com.my; level 6, Pavilion KL, 168 Jln Bukit Bintang; tickets RM11-20; 🚇AirAsia-Bukit Bintang)

TGV Cineplex   CINEMA

Take your pick from the mainstream offerings at this 12-screen multiplex (see **35** 🅰 Map p30, E2). Book in advance or be prepared to queue, particularly at weekends. (www.tgv.com.my; 3rd fl, Suria KLCC, Jln Ampang; adult/child RM14/9; 🚇KLCC)

Live House   LIVE MUSIC

31 ⭐ Map p30, H5

This excellent new live-music and comedy venue on TREC's Electric Blvd hosts regular stand-up gigs by international comedians as well as bands and DJs. Also serves tasty Southern-style soul food (fried chicken, burgers and wraps) by the popular burger makers KGB.Get a taxi from AirAsia-Bukit Bintang. (📞012-372 2374; www.facebook.com/livehousekl; TREC, 436 Jln Tun Razak; RM30; 🕐noon-3pm & 6pm-3am Mon-Wed, to 5am Thu & Fri, 6pm-5am Sat, to 3am Sun; AirAsia-Bukit Bintang)

Chinese New Year decorations, Pavilion KL

Shopping

Pavilion KL MALL

32 🔒 Map p30, E5

Pavilion sets the gold standard in KL's shopping scene. Amid the many familiar international brands, there are some good local options, including **British India** (www.britishindia.com.my) for fashion, offering well-made linen, silk and cotton clothing for men and women; and the more affordable Padini Concept Store. For a quick trip to Japan, head to the Tokyo Street of stalls on the 6th floor. (www.pavilion-kl. com; 168 Jln Bukit Bintang; ⊙10am-10pm; 🚇AirAsia-Bukit Bintang)

Royal Selangor ARTS & CRAFTS

This well-regarded chain of handcrafted pewter claims origins in 1885 when a Chinese pewtersmith arrived during KL's tin-mining boom. You can still find old pieces in Central Market antique shops but the newer works on sale in the Pavilion KL store (see 32 🔒 Map p30, E5) are outstanding. If you have time, visit the factory and visitor centre (p129), located 8km northeast of the city centre. (www. royalselangor.com; level 3, Pavilion KL, 168 Jln Bukit Bintang; ⊙10am-10pm; 🚇AirAsia-Bukit Bintang)

Khoon Hooi FASHION & ACCESSORIES

Interesting fabric textures are a signature of this Malaysian designer's work (see 34 Map p30, E5). What sets his clothes apart is attention to detail, such as pleated belts made from zips or shifts sewn from lace. (www.khoonhooi.com; Explore Fl, Starhill Gallery, 181 Jln Bukit Bintang; ⊙10am-10pm; ⊒AirAsia-Bukit Bintang)

Kinokuniya BOOKS

Kinokuniya (see **35** Map p30, E2) is the kind of bookshop where you can lose hours browsing the covetable stationery supplies and excellent selection of English-language titles, as well as books in all the other major languages of Malaysia. The upper-floor cafe has great views. (www.kinokuniya.com; level 4, Suria KLCC, Jln Ampang; ⊙10am-10pm; ⊒KLCC)

Prototype Gallery ART

33 Map p30, E2

Search out this small gallery of local arts products, ranging from 3D-printed items to prints and magazines, for the chance to see the awesome murals painted on the ceilings of this old-school mall. (www.facebook.com/prototypegallery; level 2, Wisma Central, Jln Ampang; ⊙10am-6pm Tue & Thu-Sat; ⊒KLCC)

Starhill Gallery MALL

34 Map p30, E5

With its design crossing Louis Vuitton with Louis XIV, and a basement restaurant 'village' that's a maze of dark cobbled alleys, grey slate walls and bamboo partitioning, this upscale mall is worth popping into just for a look. Fashion outlets such as Alexander McQueen are also here, as well as an excellent culinary school, and a 'Pamper' floor for spas. (www.starhillgallery.com; 181 Jln Bukit Bintang; ⊙10am-10pm; ⊒AirAsia-Bukit Bintang)

Suria KLCC MALL

35 Map p30, E2

Even if shopping bores you to tears, you're sure to find something to interest you at this fine shopping complex at the foot of the Petronas Towers. It's mainly international brands but you'll also find some local retailers here too including Royal Selangor for pewter, Vincci for shoes and accessories, and Ascana for designer fashion. (☎03-2382 2828; www.suriaklcc.com.my; KLCC, Jln Ampang; ⊙10am-10pm; ⊒KLCC)

Top Tip
Shopping Discounts

Go to concierge desks in each of the major malls to sign up for free discount shopping cards that may entitle you to free gifts and can often save you 10% or more on prices at many of the mall's outlets.

Understand

Mall City

It's hard not to get the impression that in KL, the mall rules. Malaysian consumer culture achieves its zenith in this city, where you could spend all day browsing glitzy air-conditioned malls in search of designer fashion and bargains. The scene can be exciting and innovative and most malls contain plenty of local products, from designer clothing to pewterware, and even museums, art galleries and festivals.

Bukit Bintang is the city's star spot for shopping, with Pavilion (p46), Starhill Gallery (p47) and **Lot 10** (www.lot10.com.my; 50 Jln Bukit Bintang; ⊙10am-10pm; ⊒AirAsia-Bukit Bintang) all just moments away from each other. If those malls aren't enough, a covered pedestrian walkway connects Bukit Bintang with KLCC and the Suria KLCC (p47) mall.

Outside the city centre there are yet more malls to explore. Like a fortress island surrounded by concentric moats of highways and rail tracks, Mid Valley is a two-tower complex south of Brickfields anchored by two giant malls: **Mid Valley Megamall** (www.midvalley.com.my; Lingkaran Syed Putra; ⊙10am-10pm; ⊒Mid Valley) and its luxe sibling **Gardens Mall** (www.thegardensmall.com.my; Lingkaran Syed Putra; ⊙10am-10pm; ⊒Mid Valley). The KL Komuter Mid Valley station makes getting here a cinch. You could easily lose yourself here for a day or two: it's an ideal place to head if there's a tropical downpour or you just need to escape the heat for a few hours of air-con shopping, but do avoid it on the weekends and holidays if you're not into crowds.

Art, shopping, dining and social life are all in harmony at **Publika** (www.facebook.com/PublikaGallery; 1 Jln Dutamas, Solaris Dutamas; ⊙10am-9pm), a forward-thinking retail development less than 10 minutes' drive north of KL Sentral. Contemporary art is fostered at several independent galleries, with **MAP** (☑03-6207 9732; www.facebook.com/mapkl; Publika, 1 Jln Dutamas, Solaris Dutamas; ⊙10am-9pm) acting as the cultural anchor hosting a wide variety of performances, talks and art exhibitions – everything from Malaysian death-metal bands to major public events and product launches. Free films are screened each Monday in the central square and a handicrafts is market held on the last Sunday of the month.

Lanterns, Mid Valley Megamall

Aseana
FASHION & ACCESSORIES

Billed as Malaysia's 'largest luxury multibrand boutique', Aseana (see **35** Map p30, E2) is noted for accessories, bags and jewellery. It also boasts an extensive selection from international and local fashion luminaries, such as Malaysian Farah Khan (www.farahkhan.com), who specialises in beaded and sequinned glamour wear. (www.melium.com; ground level, Suria KLCC, Jln Ampang; ☺10am-10pm; 🚇KLCC)

Avenue K
MALL

36 🔒 Map p30, E1

Anchored by a huge branch of fast-fashion retailer H&M, Avenue K has undergone a serious revamp in recent years and is now packed with shops and appealing places to eat, as well entertainment such as the interactive prehistoric exhibition **Discoveria** (📞03-2181 7218; www.discoveria.com.my; adult/child RM40/50; ☺11am-6pm Mon-Fri, 10am-8pm Sat & Sun; 👪) and a branch of the escape game Breakout. (www.avenuek.com.my; 156 Jln Ampang; ☺10am-10pm; 🚇KLCC)

Local Life
Pudu

Getting There

Pudu is within easy walking distance south of Bukit Bintang.

🚝 Pudu, then a three-minute walk to the market.

🚈 Hang Tuah; get off here to reverse walk.

Literally on the other side of the (monorail) tracks from the glitzy streets of Imbi, this largely Chinese neighbourhood is an excellent place to engage with KL's local urbanites. Start with the frenetic public wet market, then wander the back streets, exploring clusters of venerable shophouses, hawker centres and traditional industries.

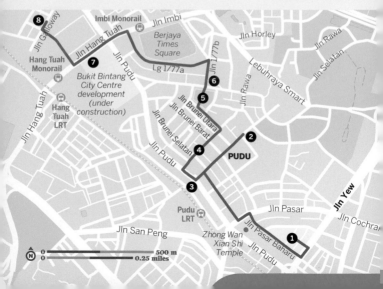

1 Pudu Market

Arrive early to experience KL's largest wet (produce) **market** (Pasar Besar Pudu; Jln Pasar Baharu; ⏱4am-2pm) at its most frantic. On Jln Yew at the market's edge, check out the row of incense, joss paper and god statuary shops. Then head to humble Zhong Wan Xian Shi Temple to see where these items are used for worship.

2 ICC Pudu

The famous Imbi Market vendors now dish up tasty breakfasts at their new home, the ground floor of the **Integrated Commercial Complex** (Jln 1/77C; dishes RM5-10; ⏱6am-2pm) in Pudu. Several stalls are located in the *kopitiam* (coffee shop) Ah Weng Koh Hainan Tea, on the right-hand side immediately after the main entrance.

3 Sek Yuen Restaurant

Occupying the same beautiful, time-worn, art deco building for the past 60 years, **Sek Yuen** (📞03-9222 0903; 315 Jln Pudu; mains RM30-45; ⏱noon-2.30pm & 5.30-9pm Tue-Sun) is a Pudu institution. Some of the aged chefs toiling in the wood-fired kitchen have served three generations the same Cantonese dishes.

4 Jalan Brunei

This short street and its intersecting alleys rewards the casual wanderer. Head down Jln Brunei Selatan and Jln Brunei Barat for prewar shophouses and inviting *kopitiam*. On Jln Brunei Utara check out **Restoran 168** (dishes from RM6; ⏱6am-4.30pm Tue-Sun), a hole-in-the-wall famous for curry laksa and *wan tan mee* (wonton noodles).

5 Eu Yan Sang

Eu Kong opened his first Yan Sang (meaning 'caring for mankind') Chinese medicine shop in Malaysia in 1879. In addition to the company's herbal remedies, the Shaw Parade **outlet** (www.euyansang.com.my; Shaw Parade, Jln Changkat Thambi Dollah; ⏱9.30am-6.30pm) includes a clinic for traditional *tuina* massage (body/foot RM88/56) and Chinese medicine.

6 Keong Kee

This **hawker stall** (cnr Jln Changkat Thambi Dollah & Jln 1/77b; dishes RM7-10; ⏱4-10.30pm Mon-Sat), set under a spreading tree in the lot across from Shaw Parade, is a Pudu institution. Try the coconut herbal curry served in a coconut shell.

7 Pudu Prison Gate

Pudu Prison was built in the late 1890s, when the area was still largely jungle. It was torn down in 2012, leaving only the gate you'll pass by as a landmark. The site is now being redeveloped as yet another mall and residential complex.

8 VCR

Set in an airy prewar shophouse, **VCR** (📞03-2110 2330; www.vcr.my; 2 Jln Galloway; ⏱8.30am-11pm; 📶) serves excellent all-day breakfast, desserts and specialty coffee. Behind the shop check out Jln Sin Chew Kee, a photogenic row of colourful shophouses that look across to Bukit Bintang.

Explore

Chinatown & Merdeka Square

You don't have to look too hard to find traces of old KL in Chinatown's shophouse-lined streets, which border the confluence of the Klang and Gombak rivers. This is where the city was born, reached its teenage years with the development of Chinatown, and celebrated its late 20s with the establishment of the British colonial ensemble around Merdeka Square.

The Sights in a Day

☀ Start the day with a fusion breakfast at **LOKL Coffee Co** (p66), then walk over to **Merdeka Square** (p54) to admire the historic buildings. On Monday, Wednesday and Saturday join the **heritage walk** (p62), otherwise stop in at the **KL City Gallery** (p62) for a rundown on the city's history. Be sure to take a look around **Masjid Jamek** (p60).

☀ Next head over to Chinatown. Stop for lunch at the **Madras Lane hawker stalls** (p66), before spending the afternoon visiting Chinatown's colourful places of worship: **Sin Sze Si Ya Temple** (p60), **Sri Mahamariamman Temple** (p56) and **Guandi Temple** (p61).

☽ Have dinner at **Merchant's Lane** (p65). Go souvenir shopping at the **Central Market** (p61), then push your way through the crowds at Chinatown's **Petaling Street Market** (p70). Finish up with a cocktail at speakeasy-style bars **PS150** (p68) or **Omakase + Appreciate** (p68).

👁 Top Sights

Merdeka Square (p54)

Sri Mahamariamman Temple (p56)

💜 Best of Kuala Lumpur

Cocktail Bars
Omakase + Appreciate (p68)

PS150 (p68)

For Free
Sri Mahamariamman Temple (p56)

Sin Sze Si Ya Temple (p60)

Masjid Jamek (p60)

National Textiles Museum (p62)

Merdeka Square (p54)

Museum of Ethnic Arts (p70)

Guandi Temple (p61)

Getting There

🚈 **LRT** Pasar Seni and Masjid Jamek LRT stations are the most convenient for the area.

🚌 **Bus** Free GO-KL City Buses ease connections between Chinatown, Bukit Nanas and Bukit Bintang.

🚇 **MRT** New stations Pasar Seni and Merdeka set to open in 2017.

Top Sights
Merdeka Square

The large, grassy square where Malaysian independence was declared in 1957 is ringed by heritage buildings and dominated by an enormous flagpole and fluttering Malaysian flag. Come here to learn about the city's history and to admire the grand colonial architecture.

History

Back at KL's founding in the mid-19th century, this patch of land west of the Gombak river was used by the tin prospectors and other settlers to grow fruit and vegetables. In 1884, after the

Dataran Merdeka

Map p58, A2

🚇 Masjid Jamek

Sultan Abdul Samad Building

founding of the Selangor Club, the land was transformed into a games pitch and was called the Padang (meaning field).

For the next 70-odd years the Padang remained the green nucleus of colonial power on the Malay Peninsula, a place for cricket, parades and civic celebrations. It became cemented in the national consciousness at midnight on 31 August 1957 when the Union flag was lowered and the Malayan States' flag hoisted on the Padang's 95m flagpole.

In 1989 the square was renamed Dataran Merdeka (Independence Square).

Heritage Buildings

Many of the colonial buildings that ring the square were designed by AC Norman, who arrived in Kuala Lumpur from England in 1883 and was appointed the government's official architect in 1890. His designs include the handsome former Standard Charter Bank building dating from 1891, which now houses a **music museum** (www. jmm.gov.my; admission free; ⊙9am-6pm).

Gracing the east side of the square are the Moorish domes and 41m clock tower of the **Sultan Abdul Samad Building**. This glorious brick building, dramatically illuminated at night, was constructed as the secretariat for the colonial administration in 1897. It's another of AC Norman's designs.

When it came to **St Mary's Anglican Cathedral** (☏03-2692 8672; www.stmaryscathedral.org.my), AC Norman stuck with the traditional blueprint of an English country church.

Built in mock Tudor style and founded in 1884, the exclusive **Royal Selangor Club** (www.rscweb.my) remains a refuge for the KL elite.

☑ Top Tips

▶ Join the free walking tour (p62) offered by Visit KL and you'll also gain access to the Royal Selangor Club, one of KL's most exclusive private member clubs.

▶ Start at the KL City Gallery (p62) to get a quick overview of the city's history and see the huge scale model of the city created by ARCH Kuala Lumpur.

✗ Take a Break

Refuel with a plate of *nasi lemak* or some cake at **ARCH Cafe** (www. klcitygallery.com; 27 Jln Raja, Merdeka Sq; mains RM10-18; ⊙9am-6.30pm; ☏) at the KL City Gallery.

Stop for healthy salads, Malaysian dishes and tempting desserts at the Canteen by Chef Adu (p66) on the ground floor of the National Textiles Museum.

Top Sights
Sri Mahamariamman Temple

This venerable Hindu shrine – the oldest in Malaysia and rumoured to be the richest – was founded by the Pillai family from the Indian state of Tamil Nadu in 1873. For 50 years it was their private shrine until opening to the public in the 1920s. Today, flower-garland vendors crowd the entrance and the temple is crowned by a five-tiered *gopuram* (temple tower), built in 1972 and covered in riotously colourful statues of Hindu deities. Passing through the gate symbolises the move from the material to the spiritual world.

Map p58, C6

163 Jln Tun HS Lee

admission free

⏲6am-8.30pm

🚇Pasar Seni

The Temple

The main prayer hall has several shrines to different Hindu deities. The main shrine, found at the rear of the complex, is for Mariamman, the South Indian mother goddess, an incarnation of Durga, also known as Parvati. On the left side of the complex is a shrine to Ganesh, the elephant-headed god, and on the right is the shrine where Lord Murugan is worshipped.

Thaipusam

The temple also houses the silver chariot in which statuettes of Lord Murugan and his consorts are transported to Batu Caves during the Thaipusam festival in January or February each year, a moving, raucous and sublime display of devotion and community spirit. Lord Murugan's silver chariot takes pride of place as it makes its way to Batu Caves in a slow procession that begins around midnight and arrives some time in the early morning at the caves. Thousands of pilgrims follow the chariot, many in various states of trance.

As with Thaipusam festivals around the world, devotees of Murugan carry a *kavadi* (literally 'burden'). This burden, often a jug of milk, is an offering to Murugan for his blessings. On arrival, pilgrims carry their *kavadi* up the 272 steps to the Temple Cave where their burden is relieved by Hindu priests. Those who have pierced their flesh will have the barbs removed and the wounds treated with ash and lemon.

The exact date of Thaipusam is usually announced in the local papers, and you can also contact the Sri Mahamariamman Temple.

☑ Top Tips

▶ Take some time out to sit inside the main prayer hall and enjoy the peaceful surroundings, just steps away from the bustle of Chinatown.

▶ Non-Hindus are welcome to visit; leave your shoes at the entrance.

✗ Take a Break

Head to the nearby Madras Lane hawkers (p66) for a wide range of cheap and tasty local breakfast and lunch options eaten at alley-side plastic tables.

Take a five minute walk to the Old China Café (p66) for good-value Peranakan grub in charmingly retro surroundings.

KL Forest Eco Park

Jln Bukit Nanas

11 ✕

22 ✕

Jln Bukit Nanas

Jln Raja Chulan

10 ⊙ Telekom Museum

Jln Gereja

16 ✕

Jln Hang Lekiu

Jln Tun Perak

Jln Sultan

Lg Ampang
20 ⊙

Jln Melaka

13 ✕

19 ✕

Jln Tun HS Lee

Jln Tan Cheng Lock

Masjid Jamek LRT

Lebuh Ampang

Jln Benteng

Jln Tun Tan Siew Sing

Lebuh Pudu

2 Sin Sze Si Ya
⊙ Temple

Sungai Klang

Jln Melayu

Medan Pasar
8 ⊙

18 ✕

Lebuh Pasar Besar

Central Market
⊙ 3

Jln Hang Kasturi

Jln Tun Perak

Masjid Jamek
⊙ 1

25 ⊙

Jln Raja Laut

Jln Tun Perak

23 ⊙

Sungai Gombak

Jln Makhamah Persekutuan

National
7 ⊙ Textiles Museum

Merdeka Square
⊙

26 ⊙

KL
City 6
Gallery ⊙

Jln Raja

Jln Raja Laut

Jln Raja

Jln Kimabalu

Pudu Sentral

Jln Pudu

Jln Pudu

For reviews see

◎	Top Sights	p54
◉	Sights	p60
✕	Eating	p65
◐	Drinking	p68
⊕	Entertainment	p69
⊞	Shopping	p70

Jln Sultan

Jln Sultan

Jln Hang Jebat

Jln Cangkat Stadium

Jln Stadium

Stadium Merdeka
◉ 9

Maharajalela Monorail

Jln Maharajalela

Jln Stadium

Jln Petaling

✕ 12

Bulatan Merdeka

Jln Belfield

Jln Akar

Jln Kampong Attap

Jln Petaling
✕ 15

Jln Hang Lekir

Guandi Temple ◉ 4
Madras La ◉ 5
La Chinatown

Madras La

CHINATOWN *Wet Market*

◐ 28
◉ 21
✕ 24
17 ✕

Jln Sultan

Jln Panggong

Sri Mahamariamman Temple ◎

Jln Tun HS Lee

Jln Hang Kasturi

Benteng

Pasar Seni LRT ⊞

Sungai Klang

Jln Kinabalu

Jln Sultan Hishamuddin

Jln Tun Sambanthan

Kuala Lumpur ⊞

Jln Tugu

Jln Sultan Hishamuddin

◉ N

200 m
0.1 miles

Sights

Masjid Jamek

MOSQUE

1 ⊙ Map p58, B2

Gracefully designed in Mogul style by British architect AB Hubback, this onion-domed mosque is situated at the confluence of the Gombak and Klang rivers. At the time of research the surroundings were being landscaped as part of the River of Life project (p72) and the original steps down to the river reinstated, but by the time you read this, the renovations should be complete. You can visit the inside of the mosque, outside of prayer times; robes are available to borrow. (Friday Mosque; off Jln Tun Perak; admission free; ⊙9am-12.30pm & 2.30-4pm Sat-Thu; ⍟Masjid Jamek)

Sin Sze Si Ya Temple

TEMPLE

2 ⊙ Map p58, C4

Kuala Lumpur's oldest Chinese temple was built on the instructions of Kapitan Yap Ah Loy and is dedicated to Sin Sze Ya and Si Sze Ya, two Chinese immigrants instrumental in Yap's ascension to Kapitan status. Several beautiful objects decorate the temple, including two hanging carved panels, but the best feature is the almost frontierlike atmosphere. This is still an important temple for the community, much as it was in 1883 when 10,000 people turned out for opening day. (Jln Tun HS Lee; admission free; ⊙7am-5pm; ⍟Pasar Seni)

Understand

The City's Changing Skyline

At the southern end of Chinatown, the old Merdeka Park has been cleared and construction is under way on the controversial Merdeka PNB118 tower, which will rise up next to Stadium Merdeka and Stadium Negara by 2019 – at 682m, it will be Malaysia's tallest building. The estimated cost of the tower, slated to be the new headquarters of PNB (Malaysia's largest fund-management company and a key instrument in the government's pro-Malay affirmative-action policies), is RM5 billion, prompting accusations that the money would have been better spent on health care or education.

Meanwhile, the site of the former Pudu Prison is being redeveloped into the Bukit Bintang City Centre (BBCC) complex. The first phase, set to be complete by 2020, will include a mall (as if KL were short of them!) with a rooftop public park and concert hall, while plans to further develop the site involve the construction of an 80-storey signature tower by 2025.

Guandi Temple

Central Market

MARKET

3 ◉ Map p58, B4

This 1930s art deco building (a former wet market) was rescued from demolition in the 1980s and transformed into a tourist-oriented arts-and-crafts centre. Nonetheless, there are some excellent shops, good restaurants, and the fascinating private museum (p70) of ethnic arts in the Annexe. The adjacent Kasturi Walk – the arch is a series of *wau bulan* (moon kites) – is bordered by handsome restored shophouses. (www.centralmarket.com.my; Jln Hang Kasturi; ◷10am-10pm; ◨Pasar Seni)

Guandi Temple

TEMPLE

4 ◉ Map p58, C5

Founded in 1886, this atmospheric temple is dedicated to Guandi, a historical Chinese general known as the Taoist god of war, but more commonly worshipped as the patron of righteous brotherhoods: he is in fact patron of both police forces and triad gangs. The temple's high ceilings, red walls, tiled eaves and pointy gable ends give it a distinctive look that's great for photos. (Jln Tun HS Lee; admission free; ◷7am-5pm; ◨Pasar Seni)

Top Tip

Walking Tours

Visit KL (p146) offers a number of worthwhile free guided walking tours. The **Kuala Lumpur Heritage Trail** (Dataran Merdeka Heritage Walk; 03-2698 0332; www.visitkl.gov.my; Merdeka Sq; 9-11.30am Mon, Wed & Sat; Masjid Jamek) takes in 11 heritage sights around Merdeka Sq. On Saturdays, take the **Kuala Lumpur Night Walk** (03-2689 3819; www.visitkl.gov.my; 6.30-9pm Sat; Masjid Jamek). Starting in Chinatown, the walk loops past Masjid Jamek and Masjid India and through the packed streets of the bustling night market. Sign up for tours in advance.

Chinatown Wet Market   MARKET

5 Map p58, C5

If you want your chicken freshly plucked, this is where to get it. The market is squished in darkened alleys between Jln Petaling and Jln Tun HS Lee and it's where locals shop for their groceries. (off Jln Tun HS Lee; 7am-1pm; Pasir Seni)

KL City Gallery   MUSEUM

6 Map p58, A3

Pick up brochures at the information centre set in the former Government Printing Office (built 1898) before exploring the small exhibition on Kuala Lumpur's history. On the 2nd floor there's a fantastic large scale model

of KL (including new buildings yet to be constructed) and you can watch a short film on the past, present and future of the city. (03-2691 1382; www.klcitygallery.com; Merdeka Sq, 27 Jln Raja; RM5; 9am-6.30pm; Masjid Jamek)

National Textiles Museum   MUSEUM

7 Map p58, A3

This excellent themed museum occupies an elegant Mogul-style building originally constructed for the railway works department. The lower floors cover the history of textiles, in particular Malaysian fabrics such as *songket* (silk or cotton with gold threading), and the traditional processes and machinery used in manufacturing. Gorgeous examples of clothing and fabric abound. The upper floors cover Malaysian fabrics and design motifs in greater detail, as well as items for personal adornment such as jewellery and headgear. (Muzium Tekstil Negara; 03-2694 3457; www.muziumtekstilnegara.gov.my; Jln Sultan Hishamuddin; admission free; 9am-6pm; Masjid Jamek)

Medan Pasar   SQUARE

8 Map p58, B3

Pedestrianised Medan Pasar (which translates as Market Square) was once the heart of Chinatown. Kapitan Yap Ah Loy lived here, and in addition to holding the city's wet market, it was a place of brothels and illegal gambling dens (now long gone). In the centre

Understand

Yap Ah Loy & the Founding of Kuala Lumpur

Tin ore deposits had been mined in the interior of Selangor for decades before two nephews of the sultan of Selangor sponsored an expedition of 87 Chinese miners up the Klang river in 1857. Within a month all but 18 of the group were dead from malaria. However, sufficient tin was found around Ampang to encourage further parties of miners to follow. The jungle trading post where these prospectors alighted, at the meeting point of the Klang and Gombak rivers, was named Kuala Lumpur, meaning 'muddy confluence'.

In 1859, trader Hiu Siew set up shop in KL close to where the Central Market stands today. As more prospectors came to seek their fortunes, the backwater settlement quickly became a brawling, noisy, violent boom town, ruled by so-called 'secret societies', Chinese criminal gangs, and later *kongsi* (clan associations). In 1861 Hiu Siew was appointed by Raja Abdullah as the first Kapitan Cina (head of the Chinese community). But it is Yap Ah Loy, the third of KL's six Kapitan Cinas, who is generally credited as the city's founder.

Yap was only 17 when he left his village in southern China in search of work in Malaya. His big break was being the friend of KL's second Kapitan Cina, Liu Ngim Kong. When Liu died in 1869, Yap took over and managed within a few years to gather enough power and respect to be considered the leader of the city's previously fractured Chinese community. According to legend, Yap was able to keep the peace with just six policemen, such was the respect for his authority.

Yap amassed great wealth through his control of the tin trade as well as more nefarious activities, such as opium trading and prostitution, which thrived in the mining boom town. He founded the city's first school in 1884 and, by the time he died a year later, was the richest man in KL. A street in Chinatown is named after him and he is worshipped as a saint at the Sin Sze Si Ya Temple (p60), which he founded.

KL City Gallery (p62)

stands an art deco clock tower built in 1937 to commemorate the coronation of King George VI. (🚇Masjid Jamek)

Stadium Merdeka
HISTORIC BUILDING

9 ◉ Map p58, E8

Built for the declaration of independence in 1957, this open-air stadium is where Malaysia's first prime minister, Tunku Abdul Rahman, famously punched his fist in the air seven times shouting *'Merdeka!'* (Independence!). Other big events during its history include a boxing match between Muhammad Ali and Joe Bugner, and a concert by Michael Jackson. There are

panoramic views of the city from the grandstands and a couple of evocative photographic murals in the entrance hall. (Jln Stadium; 🚇Maharajalela)

Telekom Museum
LANDMARK

10 ◉ Map p58, D2

Housed in the beautifully renovated former telephone exchange building, this interesting museum has creatively designed displays on the history of communications in Malaysia, from the earliest stone carvings through the use of messenger elephants and carrier pigeons to the latest digital technology. Highlights include a section of the original switchboard from the 1920s with wires that had to be manually connected and photographs of the glamorous telephone operators of the 1950s who competed in the Miss Golden Voice contest. (www.muziumtelekom.com.my; Jln Raja Chulan; adult/child RM11/5; ⏱9am-5pm Mon-Fri; 🚇Masjid Jamek)

Eating

Antara Restaurant
FUSION $$$

 11 Map p58, E2

Chef Isadora Chai's new venture is Antara at Old Malaya, a row of 100-year-old colonial buildings that have been immaculately renovated to accommodate a cluster of upscale restaurants and bars. The menu is modern Malaysian with French inflections and features creative dishes such as scallop *popiah* rolled at the table using pancake wraps and tiffin tins of tasty fillings. (📞03-2078 8881; www.antararestaurant.com; lot 2 Old Malaya, 66-68 Jln Raja Chula; mains RM25-115; ⏱noon-2.30pm & 6-11.30pm; 🚇KL Tower)

Merchant's Lane
FUSION $$

 12 Map p58, D7

Look for the narrow doorway at the end of the block for the stairs leading up to this high-ceilinged charmer of a cafe with a gorgeous, plant-filled outdoor terrace. The vibe is relaxed, the staff young, hip and friendly, and the food a very tasty mash-up of Eastern and Western dishes, such as Italian chow mein. (📞03 2022 1736; www.facebook.com/merchantslane/home; level 1, 150 Jln Petaling; mains RM20-30; ⏱11.30am-10pm Mon, Tue, Thu & Fri, 9.30am-10pm Sat & Sun; 📶; 🚇Maharajalela)

Sangeetha
INDIAN $

 13 Map p58, C2

This well-run vegetarian restaurant serves lots of North Indian delights such as *idli* (savoury, soft, fermented-rice-and-lentil cakes) and *masala dosa* (rice-and-lentil crepes stuffed with spiced potatoes). From 4pm try the Punjabi *chaat* (snacks) including vegetable samosas and *pani puri* (stuffed dough balls) – perfect for afternoon munchies. (📞03-2032 3333; 65 Lg Ampang; mains RM13.50-18; ⏱8am-11pm; 🍴; 🚇Masjid Jamek)

Local Life
Bunn Choon

It's worth coming early to **Bunn Choon** (www.facebook.com/bunnchoonmy; 153 Jln Petaling; pastries RM1.40-2.50; ⏱10.30am-5pm Mon-Fri, 9am-6pm Sat; 🚇Maharajalela) to sample their egg tarts warm from the oven. Fourth-generation owner-baker Wong Kok Tong and his wife use the family's original egg tart recipe, and have branched out to create charcoal black sesame and green tea versions. If the egg tarts are sold out the pineapple sticks are pretty good, too.

Local Life
Breakfast in Chinatown

For a delicious local breakfast, head to the hawker stalls on **Madras Lane** (noodles RM5-6; ◷8am-4pm Tue-Sun; 🚇Pasar Seni). Standout operators include one offering *yong tau fu* (vegetables stuffed with tofu and fish paste). The *bak kut teh* (pork and medicinal herbs stew) and laksa stalls are also good. On Jln Petaling, **Chee Cheong Fun Stall** (cnr Jln Petaling & Jln Hang Lekir; noodles RM3-6; ◷7am-4pm Thu-Tue; 🥢; 🚇Pasar Seni) serves melt-in-the-mouth rice noodles doused in sweet and spicy sauces, or try **Hon Kee** (93 Jln Hang Lekir; congee RM6.50; ◷4am-3pm; 🚇Pasar Seni) for great Cantonese congee (rice porridge).

Ikan Panggang   HAWKER $$

14 🍴 Map p58, D5

Tuck into spicy fish and seafood dishes and luscious chicken wings from this stall labelled only Ikan Panggang (which means grilled fish) outside Hong Leong Bank. Order ahead: it generally takes 20 minutes for your foil-wrapped pouch of seafood to cook, allowing time to explore the market. (📞019-315 9448; Jln Hang Lekir; mains RM15; ◷5-11pm Tue-Sun; 🚇Pasar Seni)

Kim Lian Kee   CHINESE $$

15 🍴 Map p58, C5

Kim Lian Kee has been serving some of the city's best Hokkien mee since 1927, when Ong Kim Lian

arrived in KL from Fujian, China, and opened his first noodle stall in the city. Choose a table upstairs for a view of Petaling Street Market and air-con, or sit downstairs, alley-side. There is also a stall at Lot 10 Hutong (p29). (📞03-2032 4984; www.facebook.com/KimLianKee; 49 Jln Petaling; mains RM15-35; ◷11am-11pm; 🚇Pasar Seni)

LOKL Coffee Co   INTERNATIONAL $$

16 🍴 Map p58, D2

From its clever name and slick design to its tasty twists on comfort foods such as deep-fried Hainanese meatloaf sandwiches and dessert toasties, LOKL ticks all the right boxes. Also does great breakfasts (8am to 11am). (http://loklcoffee.com; 30 Jln Tun HS Lee; mains RM16-30; ◷8am-6pm Tue-Sun; 🛜; 🚇Masjid Jamek)

Old China Café   MALAYSIAN $$

17 🍴 Map p58, C7

Housed in an old guild hall of a laundry association, this long-running restaurant continues to not only conjure retro charm but also serve good-value Peranakan food. Try the beef rendang, the succulent Nonya fried chicken, and tasty appetisers such as the top hats (small pastries shaped like a hat and stuffed with veggies). (📞03-2072 5915; www.oldchina.com.my; 11 Jln Balai Polis; mains RM10-43; ◷11.30am-10.30pm; 🚇Pasar Seni)

Canteen By Chef Adu   MALAYSIAN $$

You'll be happy to linger over coffee in this serene space (see 7 ◉ Map p58, A3),

yled with mismatched antique fur-
iture, wood-cut screens and fabulous
extiles. *MasterChef Malaysia* judge
hef Adu's new cafe specialises in
ishes from his native state of Johor,
uch as laksa Johor and *soto ayam
ohor* (a yellow spicy chicken soup),
nd also does a mean rendang cottage
ie. (www.chefaduamran.com; National Tex-
les Museum, Jln Sultan Hishamuddin; mains
RM13-25; ۞9am-6pm; Ⓜ️Masjid Jamek)

Cafe Old Market Square
CAFE $

 18 Map p58, C3

Come for a local breakfast of Hainanese coffee, soft-boiled eggs and *kaya*
oast at this newly restored *kopitiam*
erving the same dishes as it did over

80 years ago. The original wall tiles
and mosaic floors have been scrubbed
clean, historical photographs hung
on the walls and the 2nd floor turned
into a gallery space. (☑️03-2022 2338;
www.cafeoldmarketsquare.com; 2 Medan
Pasar; mains RM2-14; ۞7am-4.30pm Mon-
Fri, to 3pm Sat; Ⓜ️Masjid Jamek)

Hong Ngek
CHINESE $

 19 Map p58, C3

This long-running Hokkien restaurant
serves expertly made fried *bee hoon*
(vermicelli noodles), ginger duck rice
and succulent pork ribs stewed in
Guinness. (50 Jln Tun HS Lee; mains RM6-
7.50; ۞10am-7pm Mon-Sat; Ⓜ️Masjid Jamek)

Understand

Street Art

Following in the wake of Penang's street-art revolution, a number of KL's
buildings have been brightened with large-scale paintings, including one by
Lithuanian artist Ernest Zacharevic. His mural of a **boy in a canoe** can be
seen on the wall of Wisma Allianz, next to a car park on Jln Gereja. On the
end of a terrace of shophouses on Jln Panggong in Chinatown, Russian artist
Julia Volchkova has painted an evocative mural of a **goldsmith**.

Other murals to look out for are the huge painting of a **boy in a tiger hat**
opposite the Muzium Telekom, artist Kenji Chai's giant **cockerel** on the side
of the Nando's building on Jln Tun Tan Cheng Lock, and the **#distinctive
creative art for life** explosion of colour overlooking a car park on Jln Imbi
opposite the Park Royal Hotel.

If the city's street art leaves you feeling inspired, join the **Kuala Lumpur
Urban Sketchers** (www.facebook.com/KLUrbanSketchers) at one of their monthly
sketching sessions. Run by artist KC Lee and his daughter, the group meets
every third Sunday of the month to draw on location. Before sketching, KC
Lee usually gives a short talk on the history of the spot, which is often a heritage building. Check the group's Facebook page to find out what's planned.

Cooking in clay pots, Chinatown

Drinking

Omakase + Appreciate
COCKTAIL BAR

20 🚇 Map p58, D1

This cosy, retro cocktail bar is one of KL's top-secret drinking spots. The expert mixologists here each have their own menu of speciality cocktails or, if nothing appeals, ask them to create a drink tailored to your tastes. Part of the fun is finding the entrance: look for the sign saying 'no admittance'. (www.facebook.com/OmakaseAppreciate; basement, Bangunan Ming Annexe, 9 Jln Ampang; ⊙5pm-1am Tue-Fri, 9pm-1am Sat; 🛜; 🚇Masjid Jamek)

PS150
COCKTAIL BAR

The southern end of Petaling St's evolution into a hip hood is helped along by PS150 (see **12** ✗ Map p58, D7), a cocktail bar concealed behind a fake toyshop in a building that was once a brothel. Inside, the dim red lights and vintage-style booths bring to mind the films of Wong Kar-Wai; the open-air courtyard and back bar are spaces in a more modern style. (📞03-2022 2888; www.ps150.my; ground fl, 150 Jln Petaling; ⊙6pm-2am Tue-Sat, 3-10pm Sun; 🚇Maharajalela)

Moontree House
CAFE

21 Map p58, C6

Apart from being a quiet space for a well-prepared hand-drip or siphon coffee in an old Chinatown shophouse, Moontree also sells cute handicrafts and feminist literature and is probably the best central place to make enquiries about KL's discreet lesbian scene. (www.moontree-house.blogspot.com; 1st fl, 6 Jln Panggong; ⊙10am-8pm Wed-Mon; ⊛; ⊟Pasar Seni)

Luna Bar
BAR

22 Map p58, E2

A twinkling view of KL's skyline is guaranteed at this sophisticated rooftop bar surrounding a swimming pool. (☎03-2332 7777; www.pacific-regency. com; 34th fl, Pacific Regency Hotel Suites, Jln Punchak, off Jln P Ramlee; ⊙5pm-1am Sun-Thu, to 3am Fri & Sat; ⊛; ⊟KL Tower)

Entertainment

Mud
THEATRE

23 Map p58, B1

This lively musical show mixes a modern multicultural Malaysia theme with historical vignettes from KL's early days. The young, talented cast give it their all and there's some fun to be had with audience participation. It's staged in a beautiful historic theatre, the intimate auditorium based on the shape of a Malaysian kite. (www.mudKL.

Local Life
Jalan Petaling Hangouts

Head to the southern end of Chinatown to tap into the neighbourhood cafe culture. At **Chocha Foodstore** (☎03-2022 1100; www.facebook.com/chocha.foodstore; 156 Jln Petaling; ⊙11am-6pm Tue-Sun; ⊟Maharajalela), an abandoned hotel has been transformed into a multifunctional hipsters' paradise, with a raw concrete and timber facade and a plant-filled courtyard featuring the original hotel tiles, where 'tea sommelier' Youn serves an extensive selection of speciality brews. Nearby, try **Aku Cafe & Gallery** (☎03-2857 6887; www.oldchina.com. my; 1st fl, 8 Jln Panggong; ⊙11am-8pm Tue-Sun; ⊛; ⊟Pasar Seni), for good hand-drip coffee, cakes and desserts (try the pandan panna cotta).

---

com; Panggung Bandaraya, Jln Raja; tickets RM80; ⊙performances 3pm & 8.30pm; ⊟Masjid Jamek)

Findars
LIVE MUSIC

24 Map p58, C6

Check the Facebook page of this edgy, graphic arts space for details of gigs by local and visiting musicians and performance artists – they often happen on the weekends. The quirky street-art-style cafe-bar is an installation in itself, complete with Darth Vader mask. (www.facebook.com/FINDARS; 4th fl, 8c Jln Panggong; ⊟Pasar Seni)

Q Local Life
Chin Woo Stadium
This historic sports **stadium**
(📞03-2072 4602; www.chinwoo.org.my;
Jln Hang Jebat; swimming adult/child
RM5/2; ⏰2-8pm Mon-Fri, 9am-8pm Sat
& Sun; 🚇Pasar Seni) sits atop a hill
overlooking Chinatown. The highlight here is its 50m outdoor pool. If
you're keen to take a dip, note that
all swimsuits must be tight-fitting,
ie no baggy shorts even with an
inner mesh lining, and you need
a cap.

Shopping

Gahara Galleria   CLOTHING
This boutique at the National Textiles
Museum (see 7 ◉ Map p58, A3) sells
pieces by the Malaysian label Ruzz
Gahara. Batik artisans – many of them
based in the villages of rural Kelantan – use traditional printing methods
to create the textiles from which Ruzz
Gahara's beautiful contemporary designs are made. And since the textiles
are hand-printed, no two garments
are exactly alike. (www.ruzzgahara.com;
National Textiles Museum, 26 Jln Sultan Hishamuddin; ⏰10am-6pm Mon-Fri, 11am-5pm Sat
& Sun; 🚇Masjid Jamek)

Museum of Ethnic Arts   ANTIQUES
25 🔒 Map p58, B4

Although billed as a museum,
almost everything is for sale in this
extraordinary private collection of
tribal arts from Borneo. You'll also
find Nonya ceramics, Tibetan thangka
paintings, Chinese paintings and
porcelain, embroidered wall hangings,
hand-carved boxes and doors, and
all manner of delights from Malaysia
and the region. There's also a gallery
of contemporary artworks. (📞03-2301
1468; 2nd fl, the Annexe, 10 Jln Hang Kasturi;
⏰11am-7pm; 🚇Pasar Seni)

Asli Craft   ARTS & CRAFTS
Beautiful items for sale in the Central
Market (see 3 ◉ Map p58, B4), handmade
by Malaysia's different indigenous
groups including rattan baskets and
beaded purses from Sarawak, Mah
Meri headpieces, blowpipes and fish-
trap bamboo lampshades. (G23 ground fl,
main building, Central Market, Jln Hang Kasturi;
⏰10am-9.30pm; 🚇Pasar Seni)

House of Rinpo   ANTIQUES
26 🔒 Map p58, A3

In the underground mall at the southern end of Merdeka Sq is this small
antique shop run as a hobby by af-
fable Uncle Khoo. The quality of items
varies but there are usually some good
finds to be had among the ceramics,
paintings, and daily life items from
the past. (C30, Dataran Underground,
Merdeka Sq; ⏰10am-6pm; 🚇Masjid Jamek)

Petaling Street Market   MARKET
27 🔒 Map p58, C5

Malaysia's relaxed attitude towards
counterfeit goods is well illustrated
at this heavily hyped night market

Cooking steamed buns, Chinatown

brackcted by fake Chinese gateways. Traders start to fill Jln Petaling from midmorning until it is jam-packed with market stalls selling everything from fake Mulberry handbags to jackfruit. Visit in the afternoon if you want to take pictures or see the market without the crowds. (Jln Petaling; ⊙10am-10.30pm; 🚇Pasar Seni)

Rhino
ARTS & CRAFTS

Charming hand-painted clogs and handicrafts (see 3 ⊙ Map p58, B4). The soles of the shoes are made from the wood of thc durian tree. (KB17 ground fl, main bldg, Central Market, Jln Hang Kasturi; ⊙9am-10.30pm; 🚇Pasar Seni)

Songket Sutera Asli
ARTS & CRAFTS

Fine-quality decorative weavings and embroidery in silver and gold thread (see 3 ⊙ Map p58, B4). (M53 mezzanine fl, main bldg, Central Market, Jln Hang Kasturi; ⊙10am-9.30pm; 🚇Pasar Seni)

Tanamera
COSMETICS

Malaysian-brand spa products made from 100% natural materials, including detox infusions, essential oils and various balms (see 3 ⊙ Map p58, B4). (www.tanamera.com.my; G25 ground fl, main bldg, Central Market, Jln Hang Kasturi; ⊙10am-9.30pm; 🚇Pasar Seni)

Understand

River of Life

The literal translation of Kuala Lumpur is 'muddy estuary' and anyone gazing on any of the milky-coffee-coloured waterways that flow through the city would still find that name appropriate. But following successes in Melaka and Penang on cleaning up polluted rivers, the focus has now turned to KL, where the RM4 billion River of Life project involves transforming the Klang river from a polluted sinkhole into a clean and liveable waterfront, with parks and other beautification efforts. The aim is to clean up a 110km stretch along the Klang river basin, shifting the water quality from Class III–Class V status (not suitable for body contact) to Class IIb (suitable for body-contact recreational usage) by 2020.

The first phase of the project has centred on improvements in Chinatown, by widening pavements, brightening the streets with statues by local artists and improved signage, and pedestrianising Medan Pasar. The original steps down to the river behind Masjid Jamek (p60), once used to access the building by boat, have been uncovered and reinstated. They form an elegant addition to the view of the mosque from the adjoining riverbank, which has also been done-up as part of the project. A pedestrian bridge will link Masjid Jamek with Merdeka Sq, while the entrance to the mosque will be fronted by a landscaped plaza with shaded areas and fountains.

A number of sculptures have been commissioned, including red-painted metal sculptures by Kuen Stephanie depicting scenes from Malaysian life in the style of paper cuttings. These can be seen on Bangkok Bank Sq and Lebuh Pudu. Fun, life-size sculptures based on cartoonist Lat's humorous characters are dotted along the trail from Jln Melaka to the KL Forest Eco Park on Jln Raja Chulan.

Next up is the redevelopment of the riverbank south of Chinatown to Mid Valley, with pocket parks planned in the Brickfields area as well as cycle paths and bicycle-rental stations along the way.

Petaling Street Market (p70)

Wau Tradisi
ARTS & CRAFTS

Has an eye-catching selection of traditional paper and bamboo kites, including the giant *wau bulan* (moon kite) from Kelantan (see **3** ◉ Map p58, B4). (M51 mezzanine fl, main bldg, Central Market, Jln Hang Kasturi; ⏰10am-9.30pm; 🚇Pasar Seni)

Purple Cane Tea Arts
TEA

28 🔒 Map p58, C6

One of several specialist tea shops in Chinatown where you can sample and buy Chinese teas (mostly Pu-erh) and all manner of tea-making paraphernalia. (www.purplecane.com.my; 11 Jln Sultan; ⏰10am-9pm; 🚇Pasar Seni)

Explore

Masjid India & Kampung Baru

Surrounding the mosque of the same name, Masjid India is not to be missed for its Saturday night market. To the east are the traditional wooden houses of Kampung Baru, a Malay village within the heart of the modern city. Chow Kit hosts a wonderful wet market, while further north is leafy Lake Titiwangsa, providing respite from the city.

The Sights in a Day

☀ Take the monorail to **Titiwangsa Lake Gardens** (p78), a popular spot for strolling and taking snaps of the city's skyline. Visit the nearby **National Visual Arts Gallery** (p78) to see the latest contemporary Malaysian art exhibitions, and check if there are any interesting shows worth taking in at **Istana Budaya** (p86).

☀ Head back into town for lunch at **Yut Kee** (p83), an old-school Hainanese *kopitiam* (coffee shop). Then take a taxi to **Bank Negara Malaysia Museum & Art Gallery** (p78), where a collection of small galleries offer a visual take on money. Afterwards, head to the atmospheric wet market **Bazaar Baru Chow Kit** (p84) and slowly make your way to **Kampung Baru** (p78). If it's Tuesday, Thursday or Sunday take the Visit KL **walking tour** (p78); otherwise follow ours (p122).

☾ Make your way to the Row for dinner at **Limapulo** (p83) then wander over for a nightcap at **Coliseum Cafe** (p85), once a favourite haunt of Somerset Maugham.

♥ Best of Kuala Lumpur

Hawker Food
Kin Kin (p82)

Kopitiam
Yut Kee (p83)

Capital Cafe (p84)

Market Food
Bazaar Baru Chow Kit (p84)

Masjid India Pasar Malam (p84)

Heritage Buildings
Loke Mansion (p82)

Sultan Sulaiman Club (p80)

Getting There

🚝 **Monorail** Convenient stops for this area are Medan Tuanku, Chow Kit and Titiwangsa.

🚈 **LRT** The Ampang and Kelana Jaya lines have stations in these areas.

🚉 **KTM Komuter** Take the Batu Caves line to Bank Negara and Sentul.

🚌 **Bus** The GOKL City Bus red line goes to Titiwangsa and Chow Kit. The blue line goes to Medan Tuanku monorail station.

Titwangsa
Lake Gardens

Jln Tembeling

TITIWANGSA

Lake
Titiwangsa

National
Visual Arts
Gallery 2

Jln Temerloh

KL Sky
Tour 4

Jln Raja Muda Abdul Aziz

Jln Haji Yahya Sheik Ahmad

Jln Hamzah

21

Jln Kuantan

Jln Tun Razak

Jln Daud

Raja Abdullah

23

D

Persiaran Titiwangsa 3

Jln Pahang

Hospital
Kuala
Lumpur

Jln Raja Uda

C

Jln Pahang

Chow Kit
Monorail

Haji Hussein

Jln Chow Kit

**CHOW
KIT**

Titiwangsa
LRT

Titiwangsa
Monorail

Sungai Gombak

Jln Ipoh

Jln Tun Razak

PWTC
LRT

Sungai Batu

Jln Putra

Jln Ipoh

Putra

500 m
0.25 miles

N
0
0

For reviews see

◉	Sights	p78
✕	Eating	p82
◐◑◒	Drinking	p85
✦✧	Entertainment	p86
▣	Shopping	p87

A   B   C   D   E

1

2

3

4

Kampung Baru LRT

Jln Raja Mahwa Musa

Jln Raja Alang

Baru

Sungai Klang

Ampang Elevated Hwy

Muslim Cemetery

10

18

Jln Ampang

Jln Parak

Jln Sultan Ismail

Jln P Ramlee

Bukit Nanas Monorail

Jln Punchak

Jln Punchak

KL Forest Eco Park

E

13

Jln Raja Abdullah

Sultan Sulaiman Club

6

Dang Wangi LRT

D

Tatt Khalsa Diwan Gurdwara

Jln OS Sulaiman

Jln Sultan Ismail

Jln Kamunting

14

Jln Bukit Nanas

Medan Tuanku Monorail

11

25

Jln Tuanku Abdul Rahman (T.

Jln Doraisamy

12

24

20

Jln Munshi Abdullah

Jln Ampang

Masjid Jamek LRT (200m)

C

Loke Mansion

8

Jln Medan Tuanku

Jln Dang Wangi

Jln Masjid India

Lg TAR

17

26

Masjid India

Jln Tuanku Abdul Rahman (TAR)

5

B

Bandaraya LRT

Sultan Ismail LRT

Jln Raja Laut

15

Lg TAR

16

19

22

Jln Raja Laut

Jln Tiong N

Jln Kuching

Sungai Gombak

Jln Dato Onn

n Kuching

3

Bank Negara Malaysia Museum & Art Gallery

A

5

6

7

8

Sights

Kampung Baru

AREA

1 ◎ Map p76, D5

The charm of this Malay area, gazetted by the British in the 1890s, lies in just wandering the streets, which you can also do with a guide on the city's free Kampung Baru walking tour. Traditional Malay wooden houses stand amid leafy gardens and people go quietly about their daily lives as they have done for decades. Along the way enjoy tasty home-cooked Malay food at unpretentious roadside cafes and stalls. Sign up for the free **Kampung Baru walking tour** (Jalan-Jalan at Kampong Bharu; ☏03-2698 0332; www.visitkl. gov.my/visitklv2; ⏰4.15-7.15pm Tue, Thu &

Sun; 🚇Medan Tuanku) from Visit KL. The route takes in not only the neighbourhood sights but also traditional shops, popular dishes and food venues, and Malay customs. Tours start at the Sultan Sulaiman Club.(🚇Kampung Baru)

National Visual Arts Gallery

GALLERY

2 ◎ Map p76, E2

Occupying a pyramid-shaped block, the NVAG showcases modern and contemporary Malaysian art. It's always worth turning up to see a variety of interesting temporary shows of local and regional artists, as well as pieces from the gallery's permanent collection of 4000 pieces, including paintings by Zulkifli Moh'd Dahalan, Wong Hoy Cheong, Ahmad Fuad Osman and the renowned batik artist Chuah Thean Teng. On the ground floor, the National Portrait Gallery hosts regularly changing exhibitions. (NVAG, Balai Seni Lukis Negara; ☏03-4026 7000; www. artgallery.gov.my; 2 Jln Temerloh; admission free; ⏰10am-6pm; 🚇Titiwangsa)

Bank Negara Malaysia Museum & Art Gallery

MUSEUM

3 ◎ Map p76, A7

This well-designed complex of small museums focuses on banking, finance and money and is not dull in the least. Highlights include a collection of ancient coins and money (and a slick interactive screen to examine their history), a gallery of the bank's private art collection, a surreal 3m-

---

> **Q** Local Life
>
> ### Titiwangsa Lake Gardens
>
> For a postcard-perfect view of the city skyline, head to **Lake Titiwangsa** (Taman Tasik Titiwangsa; Jln Tembeling; 🚇Titiwangsa) and the relaxing tree-filled park that surrounds it. If you're feeling energetic, hire a **motor boat** (☏03-7733 4181; www.tubesterinc.com; 20-min rides adult/child RM35/25; ⏰10am-7pm Tue-Fri, 9am-7.30pm Sat & Sun), go for a jog, hire a bike, play some tennis or even go for a spin in a helicopter. The park is a favourite spot for courting Malaysian couples. It's a 10-minute walk east of the monorail station.

Kampung Baru

long tunnel lined with RM1 million (in the Children's Gallery), and a history of the Islamic banking system (which must comply with sharia law, including prohibitions against usury). (☏03-9179 2784; www.museum.bnm.gov.my; Sasana Kijang, 2 Jln Dato Onn; admission free; ◷10am-6pm; ☒Bank Negara)

KL Sky Tour
SCENIC FLIGHTS

4 ◉ Map p76, D1

Departing from a helipad on the edge of Titiwangsa lake, KL's new helicopter tours allow you to swing between the city's skyscrapers in style. A six-minute whizz around the lake gardens will set you back RM600 for up to three people; if you go for the 15-minute tour (RM1500) you'll get as far as Batu Caves. (☏03-7845 467; www.cempaka.com.my; Titiwangsa Helipad, Titiwangsa Lake Gardens; 6/15/30/45min tours for up to 3 people RM600/1500/3000/4500; ◷10am-6pm; ☒Titiwangsa)

Masjid India
MOSQUE

5 ◉ Map p76, B8

The original wooden mosque that gave the area its name was built in 1883, and replaced by a bulky red-granite tiled modern structure in 1963. It's not much to look at, and you can't go inside, but it's fronted by a busy market and surrounded by stalls selling religious items and traditional Malay costumes. (Jln Masjid India; ☒Masjid Jamek)

Textiles for sale, Jalan Masjid India

Sultan Sulaiman Club
HISTORIC BUILDING

6 ⊙ Map p76, D5

Dating back to 1901, this is the oldest Malay club in KL and is said to be where the meetings took place that led to the foundation of the United Malays National Organisation (UMNO; the lead party in the ruling coalition). The original club building was demolished in the late '60s. In 2007 a local architectural firm constructed an exact replica, which is located across from the new club at the back of a field. (Bangunan Warisan Kelab Sultan Suleiman; Jln Datuk Abdul Razak; 🚇Kampung Baru, 🚇Medan Tuanku)

Tatt Khalsa Diwan Gurdwara
SIKH TEMPLE

7 ⊙ Map p76, C5

This is the largest Sikh temple in Southeast Asia and the spiritual home of KL's 75,000 Sikhs. There's been a temple and school here since 1924, though the present building dates from the 1990s. Visitors are welcome to enter and see the main shrine with a guide but they must wear a headscarf (headwrap for men, which will be provided at the entrance) and pants or a long dress. There's a free vegetarian lunch on Sundays, open to all visitors. (24 Jln Raja Alang; admission free; 🚇Chow Kit)

Understand

Colonial Architecture

Shophouses & Colonial Architecture

Thanks to fires and civil war, not to mention their own fragile nature, none of the wooden and *atap* (thatch) huts of the original settlers of KL have survived. However, from the 1880s onwards the city was built in brick, with tiled roofs and stucco facades. Grand civic buildings such as those around Merdeka Sq signalled the British desire to stamp their colonial mark on the city. It's also from this era that KL's first brick shophouses started appearing, some of which can still be found along Jln Tun HS Lee.

Shophouses are exactly what they sound like – a shop at the front with living quarters above and to the rear. Constructed in terraces, each unit is long and narrow, approximately 6m by 24m. An open courtyard in the middle of the building provides light and ventilation. Walkways sheltered by verandas at the front provide protection from both rain and harsh sunlight.

As KL became more prosperous so did the style of shophouse architecture. Look around Chinatown and Masjid India and you'll see shophouses with Grecian pediments and columns and fancy window frames – the neoclassical style of the 1910s; Dutch inspired gables, a style from the 1920s known as Dutch Patrician; and the geometric art deco style of the 1930s. The wealthiest residents constructed palladian-style villas such as Loke Mansion (p82) and the former Istana Negara. Jln Ampang, the road leading out to the former tin mines of Ampang, used to be lined with these mansions – only a handful remain.

The Two Arthurs

Arthur Benison Hubback (1871–1948) and Arthur Charles Norman (1858–1944) are the two colonial-era architects whose fanciful Indo-Saracenic style of buildings have lent distinction to KL's cityscape since the late 19th century. Hubback is most famous for designing Masjid Jamek (p60), the graceful mosque with its Mogul domes and scalloped horseshoe arches; the spectacular old KL train station (p105); and the matching Malayan Railway Administration Building on Jln Sultan Hishamuddin. Norman was responsible for the collection of buildings around Merdeka Sq, most notably the Sultan Abdul Samad Building (p55).

Top Tip

Ramadan in Kampung Baru

If you're in town during the Muslim fasting month don't miss the Ramadan street markets in Kampung Baru (p78), where you can buy all manner of tasty delicacies to break the fast. Just remember not to start eating until after sundown.

Loke Mansion HISTORIC BUILDING

 8 Map p76, C6

Rescued from the brink of dereliction by the law firm Cheang & Ariff, Loke Mansion was once the home of self-made tin tycoon Loke Yew. The Japanese high command set up base here in 1942. After years of neglect, the mansion has been beautifully restored; access to the interior is by appointment only, but you're welcome to pause in the driveway and admire the whitewashed exterior any time. (📞03-2691 0803; 273a Jln Medan Tuanku; ⏰9am-5pm Mon-Fri; 🚇Medan Tuanku)

Masjid Jamek Kampung Baru MOSQUE

 9 Map p76, D5

Founded in the late 1880s, this is Kampung Baru's principal mosque; it has recently been expanded and sports a handsome gateway decorated with eye-catching tiles in traditional Islamic patterns. Entry is permitted outside of prayer times, as long as you are respectfully attired. (http://masjidmjkb.org.my; Jln Raja Alang; admission free; ⏰9am-noon, 3-4pm & 5.30-6.30pm; 🚇Kampung Baru)

Muslim Cemetery CEMETERY

 10 Map p76, E6

Tucked away off Jln Ampang and split from Kampung Baru by a highway is one of KL's oldest Muslim burial grounds. It's shaded by giant banyans and rain trees planted in the early 20th century. The famous film director, actor and singer P Ramlee, two of his former wives and his co-star AR Tompel are buried here. Men need to wear long trousers and women a headscarf if they wish to visit. (off Jln Ampang; ⏰7am-7pm; 🚇Bukit Nanas)

Eating

Kin Kin CHINESE $

 11 Map p76, C6

This bare-bones shop is famous throughout the city for its chilli *pan mee*. These 'dry' noodles, topped with a soft-boiled egg, minced pork, *ikan bilis* (small, deep-fried anchovies), fried onion and a special spicy chilli sauce, are a taste sensation. If you don't eat pork, staff do a version topped with mushrooms. (40 Jln Dewan Sultan Sulaiman; noodles RM7.50; ⏰8am-6.30pm Tue-Sun; 🚇Medan Tuanku)

Roti canai (flaky flatbread)

Limapulo MALAYSIAN $$

12 Map p76, C6

Its tag line is 'baba can cook', the baba being genial Uncle John who is often to be found greeting guests at this atmospheric and justly popular restaurant. The Nonya-style cooking is very homely with dishes such as *ayam pongteh* (a chicken stew) and shrimp and petai beans cooked in sambal. The set lunches are good value. (☎03-2698 3268; 50 Jln Doraisamy; mains RM17-45, set lunches RM9.90; ☺noon-3pm & 6-10pm Mon-Sat; ☒Medan Tuanku)

Ikan Bakar Berempah HAWKER $

13 Map p76, D5

This excellent barbecued-fish stall sits within a hawker-stall market covered by a zinc roof and is one of the best places to eat in Kampung Baru. Pick your fish off the grill and add *kampung*-style side dishes to it off the long buffet. (Jln Raja Muda Musa; mains RM5-10; ☺7am-10pm; ☒Kampung Baru)

Yut Kee CHINESE $

14 Map p76, C7

This beloved *kopitiam* (in business since 1928), run by a father-and-son team and their crew of friendly,

Local Life
Bazaar Baru Chow Kit

This daily **wet-and-sundry market** (Chow Kit Market; 469-473 Jln TAR; ◷8am-5pm; 🚇Chow Kit) serving the Chinese and Malay working class of Chow Kit now occupies a slick new building and the surrounding alleyways, but it hasn't lost its heady, chaotic atmosphere. Though the stalls are now easier to navigate, you'll find the same hangers loaded with fruit, veggies and freshly butchered meat, with vendors shouting their prices to drum up business. Stop for a freshly made *murtabak* (Indian-style pancake stuffed with chicken or mutton) at **Murtabak Ana** (📞012-255 5774; murtabak RM3; ◷8am-4pm).

efficient staff, serves classic Hainanese and colonial-era food: try the chicken chop, *roti babi* (French toast stuffed with pork), toast with homemade *kaya* (coconut-cream jam), or Hokkien mee. (📞03-2698 8108; 1 Jln Kamunting; meals RM6.50-16; ◷7.30am-4.30pm Tue-Sun; 🚇Medan Tuanku)

Capital Café
MALAYSIAN $

15 🍴 Map p76, B7

Since it opened in 1956, this truly Malaysian cafe has had Chinese, Malays and Indians all working together, cooking up excellent renditions of Malay classics such as mee goreng, *rojak* (salad doused in a peanut-sauce dressing) and satay

(only available in the evenings). (213 Jln TAR; dishes RM4-6; ◷7.30am-7.30pm Mon-Sat; 🚇Bandaraya)

Masjid India Pasar Malam
HAWKER $

16 🍴 Map p76, B8

From around 3pm until late every Saturday, stalls pack out the length of Lg Tuanku Abdul Rahman, the alley between Jln TAR and Masjid India. Amid the headscarf and T-shirt sellers are plenty of stalls serving excellent Malay, Indian and Chinese snacks and colourful soya- and fruit-based drinks. (Night Market; Lg Tuanku Abdul Rahman; street food RM5-10; ◷3pm-midnight Sat; 🚇Masjid Jamek)

Saravana Bhavan
INDIAN $$

17 🍴 Map p76, C8

This global chain of restaurants offers some of the best-quality Indian food you'll find in KL. Their banana-leaf and mini-tiffin feasts are supremely tasty and you can also sample southern Indian classics such as *masala dosa* (rice-and-lentil crepe stuffed with spiced potatoes). (📞03-2698 3293; www.saravanabhavan. com; Selangor Mansion, Jln Masjid India; meals RM10-20; ◷8am-10.30pm; 🍴; 🚇Masjid Jamek)

Kak Som
MALAYSIAN $

18 🍴 Map p76, D5

Specialising in east coast Peninsular Malaysian dishes such as *nasi kerabu*

(blue rice), this is a good place to dine inexpensively on the main Kampung Baru restaurant strip. Take your pick of items from the buffet along with rice and the waitstaff will come to take a drink order and tally up your bill. (Jln Raja Muda Musa; meals RM10-15; ⊙8am-3am; 🚇Kampung Baru)

Drinking

Coliseum Cafe
BAR

19 🚇 Map p76, B8

The kind of bar in which colonial planters and clerks would have knocked back stouts and G&Ts, this retro watering hole (in business since 1921) oozes nostalgia. The bar is worth visiting even if you don't eat a meal at the adjoining grill room, where little seems to have changed since Somerset Maugham tucked into its famous sizzling steaks. (www.coliseum1921.com; 100 Jln TAR; ⊙10am-10pm; 🚇Masjid Jamek)

Butter & Beans
CAFE

20 🚇 Map p76, C6

Jln Doraisamy's reinvention as the Row has thrown up a few cool cafes and restaurants to hang out in including this one, handy for cold-brew coffee and other drinks. Next door is Slate, a space where events and music performances are held. (☎03-2060 2177; www.facebook.com/butterbeans.my; 42 Jln Doraisamy; ⊙7.30am-11pm Mon-Fri, 9.30am-11pm Sat & Sun; 🚇Medan Tuanku)

Understand
Traditional Malay Architecture

Vividly painted and handsomely proportioned, traditional wooden Malay houses are also perfectly adapted to the hot, humid conditions of the region. Built on stilts, with high, peaked roofs, they take advantage of even the slightest cooling breeze. Further ventilation is achieved by full-length windows, no internal partitions, and lattice-like grilles in the walls. The layout of a traditional Malay house reflects Muslim sensibilities. There are separate areas for men and women, as well as distinct areas where guests of either sex may be entertained.

The best examples of this type of architecture in KL are found scattered across Kampung Baru, the most Malay part of the city. In the grounds of the National Museum (p102), the Forest Research Institute Malaysia (p90) and Badan Warisan Malaysia (Rumah Penghulu Abu Seman; p33) ornate examples of traditional wooden architecture have been transported from other parts of the country, reconstructed and opened for public inspection.

Shadow puppets, Istana Budaya

Entertainment

Istana Budaya   PERFORMING ARTS

 Map p76, D2

Large-scale drama and dance shows are staged here, as well as music performances by the National Symphony Orchestra and National Choir. The building's soaring roof is based on a traditional Malay floral decoration of betel leaves, while the columned interior invokes a provincial colonialism. There's a dress code of no shorts and no short-sleeved shirts. (National Theatre; ☏03-4026 5555; www.istanabudaya.gov. my; Jln Tun Razak; tickets RM100-300; 🚇Titiwangsa)

Coliseum Theatre   CINEMA

 Map p76, B8

One of KL's oldest still-functioning cinemas, this art deco–style building dates back to 1920 and screens Tamil and other Indian-language movies. (94 Jln TAR; 🚇Masjid Jamek)

Sutra Dance Theatre   DANCE

 Map p76, D1

The home of Malaysian dance legend Ramli Ibrahim has been turned into a showcase for Indian classical dance as well as a dance studio, painting and photography gallery and cultural centre near Lake Titiwangsa. See its website for upcoming events. (☎03-4021 1092; www.sutrafoundation.org.my; 12 Persiaran Titiwangsa 3; 🚇Titiwangsa)

Shopping

League of Captains   FASHION & ACCESSORIES

24 🔒 Map p76, C6

T-shirts and caps by local label Pestle & Mortar Clothing and accessories by other hip young designers are artfully displayed at this boutique. It doubles as a cafe selling excellent coffee, homemade cakes and beef rendang pie. (www.facebook.com/leagueofcaptains; Lot 42-50 The Row, Jln Doraisamy; ⊗boutique noon-9pm; 🚇Medan Tuanku)

Rattan Art Enterprises   ARTS & CRAFTS

25 🔒 Map p76, C6

Handmade rattan rocking chairs, baskets, bags and mats. (☎017-622 2530; www.gekguan.com; 343 Jln Tuanku Abdul Rahman; ⊗10am-6pm Mon-Sat, to 4pm Sun; Medan Tuanku)

Semua House   DEPARTMENT STORE

26 🔒 Map p76, B8

Two floors of Indian wedding shops can be found at this department store, right in the heart of Masjid India and the Saturday *pasar malam* (night market). The perfume section at the entrance is particularly impressive. (cnr Jln Masjid India & Jln Bunus 6; ⊗10am-10pm; 🚇Masjid Jamek)

Top Sights
Batu Caves

Getting There

🚈 The KTM Komuter terminates at Batu Caves station.

🚌 Around RM20 to RM30 from central KL.

One of Malaysia's most iconic sights and holiest Hindu shrines, this complex of giant limestone caves houses temples that have been drawing pilgrims for more than 120 years. Home to a troop of cheeky macaques, the caves are always a colourful and fascinating place to visit, especially during the festival of Thaipusam when hundreds of thousands of pilgrims converge here.

Lord Murugan statue, Temple Cave

Temple Cave

The so-called **Temple Cave** (admission free; ⊘8am-8.30pm; ᯤBatu Caves), actually two enormous caverns joined by a short flight of stairs, sits atop 272 steps populated by scampering macaque monkeys and is guarded by an impressive, 42.7m golden statue of Hindu god Lord Murugan, erected in 2006 and said to be the largest in the world. The dome-shaped cavern has been a Hindu shrine since K Thambusamy Pillai, founder of the Sri Mahamariamman Temple (p56) in KL, placed a statue of Lord Murugan here in 1890.

Inside the first cavern, Murugan's six abodes are carved into the walls. The second cavern holds the temple of Valli Devanai, Murugan's wife.

Dark Cave

At step 204 on the way up to the Temple Cave, branch off to the **Dark Cave** (☏012-371 5001; www.darkcavemalaysia.com; adult/child RM35/25; ⊘10am-5pm Tue-Fri, 10.30am-5.30pm Sat & Sun) to join an excellent, 45-minute guided tour along 850m of the 2km of surveyed passageways within the cave complex. The tour takes you through seven different chambers where you can witness dramatic limestone formations, including gorgeous flowstones, see pits used for guano extraction, and possibly spot two species of bat and hundreds of other life forms, including the rare trapdoor spider.

Ramayana Cave

Perhaps no cave at Batu is more spectacularly embellished and enjoyable to visit than the **Ramayana Cave** (RM5; ⊘8.30am-6pm), which boasts psychedelic dioramas of the Indian epic Ramayana. This cave is on the left as you come out of the train station.

☑ Top Tips

▶ To visit the Temple Cave, women must wear skirts or trousers that come below the knee. Sarongs are available to rent at the cave entrance for RM3.

▶ Bring water for the climb up to the Temple Cave, but keep any bottles or food out of sight of the monkeys.

✗ Take a Break

The best of the restaurants and food stalls on the strip to the right of the Temple Cave is **Restoran Rani** (mains RM6-12; ⊘8am-9pm; ☏); head there for good-value vegetarian thali sets, rotis and *dosas* washed down with a refreshing coconut juice served straight from the nut.

Top Sights
Forest Research Institute Malaysia (FRIM)

Getting There

🚇 KTM Komuter to Kepong Sentral, then a taxi. Arrange for the taxi to pick you up again later.

Covering nearly 600 hectares, the Forest Research Institute Malaysia (FRIM) was established in 1929 to research the sustainable management of the country's forests. As well as being an active centre for scientific research, FRIM also functions as a giant park, with quiet roads for cycling and established trails through the jungle landscape. The highlight is a fabulous canopy walkway.

Canopy walkway

Canopy Walkway

Hanging a vertigo-inducing 30m above the forest floor, the 150m-long canopy walkway takes you right into the trees, offering views of the rainforest and the towers of KL in the distance. It's reached by a steep, 900m trail from the **One Stop Centre** (📞03-6279 7649; ⏰9am-1pm & 2-5pm Mon-Thu, 9am-12.15pm & 2.45-5pm Fri, 9am-1.30pm & 2-3pm Sat & Sun), on the right off the main road 1km from the entrance gate. The return hike, incorporating the walkway, takes around two hours.

Forest Trails

If you can get a group together, it's well worth hiring one of the park's experienced and knowledgeable **guides** (📞03-6279 7045; www.frim.gov.my; FRIM; per group RM120) for a one- to two-hour tour of the three forest trails: the Salleh, Keruing and Engkabang trails.

Because the forest is planned, it has some unusual quirks; the same species of trees were usually planted together, leading to the phenomenon of 'crown shyness' (certain species of tree never touch the leaves of a nother tree of the same species). On the Salleh trail look up for the *National Geographic* shot of the canopy of kapur trees and the maze of channel-like gaps between them.

Museum

The oldest building at FRIM houses an interesting **museum** (www.frim.gov.my; admission free; ⏰9am-noon & 2-4pm Sat-Thu, 9am-noon & 3-4pm Fri) with displays explaining the five forest types endemic to Malaysia, their different wood types and how they are used. Upstairs a gallery highlights the forest-related research carried out by FRIM.

📞 03-6279 7592

www.frim.gov.my

adult/child RM5/1

⏰ 8.30am-7.30pm

☑ Top Tips

▶ The best time to walk the canopy is around 10am, which is after the morning rush and before the afternoon rains.

▶ Visitor numbers to the canopy walkway are restricted and slots sometimes sell out; make a reservation online in advance to be sure of getting a ticket.

▶ The canopy is closed when the weather is bad.

✕ Take a Break

Fancy a picnic? Bring your own supplies to the picnic spot by the Sungai Kroh waterfalls.

Head to **Cafe Kasah** (Sungai Kroh picnic area, FRIM; mains RM5-6; ⏰7am-5pm) for nasi goreng and other local fare.

Explore

Lake Gardens & Brickfields

Born of the British desire to conquer the teeming jungle and fashion it into a pleasant park, the Lake Gardens remains a lush breathing space in the heart of KL. It's mainly covered by the Tun Abdul Razak Heritage Park and is home to the Islamic Arts Museum, National Museum and Masjid Negara. KL Sentral and Brickfields are immediately south of here.

The Sights in a Day

Hit the **Royal Museum** (p102) when it opens at 9am – ask your taxi driver to take you via **Kwong Tong Cemetery** (p106). After exploring the mansion, head to the **National Museum** (p102) and next door **Orang Asli Craft Museum** (p105), and then visit the **KL Bird Park** (p103). If you're hungry, stop for lunch at the **Hornbill Restaurant** (p109).

After spending an hour or so with the birds, explore the nearby Perdana Botanical Garden at the **Tun Abdul Razak Heritage Park** (p94), and then head to the **Islamic Arts Museum** (p96). Afterwards, take the weight off your feet and indulge in afternoon tea in the luscious orchidarium of the **Colonial Cafe** (p108).

In the evening, explore the sights of Brickfields, KL's Little India, eating at one of its many excellent restaurants – **Vishal** (p108) is a good bet. Check if there's a show on at **Temple of Fine Arts** (p111), otherwise take a stroll and soak in the atmosphere. Finish with a cocktail at **Mai Bar** (p110) – you've earned it.

For a local's day in Brickfields, see p98.

 Top Sights

Tun Abdul Razak Heritage Park (p94)

Islamic Arts Museum (p96)

 Local Life

Brickfields Temples & Treats (p98)

❤ **Best of Kuala Lumpur**

Hawker Food
Little India Fountain Hawker Stalls (p99)

Museums for History
National Museum (p102)

Royal Museum (p102)

Royal Malaysian Police Museum (p105)

Cocktail Bars
Coley (p109)

Getting There

Train, monorail and LRT KL Sentral is close to both Brickfields and the Tun Abdul Razak Heritage Park.

Bus The KL Hop-On-Hop-Off bus stops at Masjid Negara, KL Bird Park, the National Monument and the National Museum. The GOKL free city bus red line stops at KL Sentral, Masjid Negara and the National Museum.

Top Sights
Tun Abdul Razak Heritage Park

Covering 173 hectares, KL's major recreational park is better known by its colonial moniker of the Lake Gardens. Ranging over undulating, landscaped hills, it's a park with something for everyone, the main attractions being the KL Bird Park (p103) and Perdana Botanical Garden. The Islamic Arts Museum (p96), National Museum (p102), Masjid Negara (p102) and National Monument (p105) also fall within the park's boundaries.

Lake Gardens

Map p100, C3

www.visitkl.gov.my

⊘7am-8pm

🚉Kuala Lumpur

Black-naped oriole, KL Bird Park (p103)

Park History

In 1888 Alfred Venning, Selangor State Treasurer, secured permission from British Resident Frank Swettenham to create a botanical garden around the small stream Sungai Bras Bras. It took more than a decade to clear and landscape the area which today stretches from Parliament House to the National Museum. The stream was dammed to give the park Sydney Lake (Tasik Perdana) – hence the name Lake Gardens.

In 2011 the park was renamed after Abdul Razak, Malaysia's second prime minister (1970–76). Abdul Razak lived in a house in the park between 1962, when he was deputy PM, and 1976, when he died; the home is now the **Memorial Tun Abdul Razak** (www.arkib.gov.my/memorial-tun-abdul-razak; Jln Perdana; admission free; ⏰10am-5.30pm Tue-Sun, closed noon 3pm Fri) museum.

Perdana Botanical Garden

The vast **Perdana Botanical Garden** (☎03-2617 6404; www.klbotanicalgarden.gov.my; admission free; ⏰7am-8pm, ♿) showcases a wide variety of native and introduced plants with sections dedicated to ferns, rare trees, trees that have lent their names to places in Malaysia, medicinal herbs, aquatic plants and so on. The gardens are well laid out with gazebos and boardwalks (be careful of rotten wood that might break underfoot), but there is only limited signage to identify the plants.

The **Hibiscus** (Taman Bunga Raya; Jln Cenderawasih; admission free; ⏰9am-6.30pm) and **Orchid** (Taman Orkid; Jln Cenderawasih; Sat & Sun RM1, Mon-Fri free; ⏰9am-6pm) gardens are adjacent to the Botanical Garden. Among the 800-odd species of orchid are Vandas and exotic hybrids.

☑ Top Tips

▶ Pick up a map of the Perdana Botanical Garden at the **information booth** (⏰6am-8pm; 🚇Masjid Jamek).

▶ A hop-on, hop-off electric tram (RM4) shuttles around the park's major attractions from 9.30am to 5pm daily.

✗ Take a Break

Head to the Bird Park's Hornbill Restaurant (p109) for Western and Malay staples, best enjoyed (with the free-flying fowl) on the wood deck overlooking the park.

For something more local, try the hawker stalls at **Kompleks Makan Tanglin** (Jln Cenderasari; meals RM5-10; ⏰7am-4pm Mon-Sat).

Top Sights
Islamic Arts Museum

On the southern edge of the Tun Abdul Razak Heritage Park, this outstanding museum houses one of best collections of Islamic decorative arts in the world. Aside from the quality of the exhibits, which include fabulous textiles, jewellery, calligraphy-inscribed pottery and scale architectural models, the building itself is a stunner, with beautifully decorated domes and glazed tile work on its facade.

Muzium Kesenian Islam Malaysia

Map p100, D3

www.iamm.org.my

Jln Lembah Perdana

adult/child RM14/7

⊙10am-6pm

☒Kuala Lumpur

Quran

The Galleries

Spread over four levels, the museum has 12 permanent galleries and two galleries for special exhibitions. Start on the 3rd floor in the **Architecture Gallery**, which has scale models of important Islamic buildings, including Islam's holiest mosque, the Masjid al-Haram in Mecca. There's also a re-creation of a mosque interior. On the same floor, in the **Quran and Manuscripts Gallery**, look for the 19th-century Qurans from Malaysia's east coast decorated in red, gold and black, as well as a full *kiswah* (an embroidered door panel from the holy Kaaba in Mecca).

Other highlights include the **Ottoman Room**, a magnificent reconstruction of an 1820s decorative room from Syria; **Chinese calligraphy scrolls**; the weft silk ikat **limar**, a fabric patterned with Islamic calligraphy and now no longer made as the tradition has died out; and **Uzbek pectoral plates**.

The Building

Flooded with natural light, the Islamic Arts Museum is a contemporary building with airy, open spaces and wall-to-ceiling glass. The vaulted, *iwan*-style entrance resembles a ceramic tapestry and is inscribed with verses from the Quran. Iranian artisans were contracted to tile the turquoise domes on the museum roof, while the building's striking internal inverted domes were constructed by craftspeople from Uzbekistan.

☑ Top Tips

▶ If you only have time to visit one museum in KL, make it this one.

▶ Set aside a couple of hours to look around the exhibits; you won't want to rush.

▶ After visiting the museum, drop in at the Masjid Negara (p102) opposite.

✗ Take a Break

Feast on Middle Eastern food at the museum's excellent **restaurant** (☎03-2270 5152; set lunches RM51.45; ⊙noon-5pm Tue-Sun, set lunch to 3pm).

In the mood for tea and cakes? For a fancy afternoon tea head to the Colonial Cafe (p108).

Local Life
Brickfields Temples & Treats

Home to KL's official 'Little India', Brickfields is a compact, colourful and multicultural area packed with excellent eateries as well as temples and churches of various denominations. The air here is heady with the scent of incense, jasmine and spices.

❶ Vivekananda Ashram

This historic **ashram** (220 Jln Tun Sambanthan; ☒KL Sentral), built in 1904, is a well-loved subject for photographers. A campaign to save the ashram led to the government granting the building national heritage status in 2016, protecting it from developers.

❷ Little India Fountain

This eye-catching **fountain** (cnr Jln Tun Sambanthan & Jln Travers; ☒KL Sentral) is

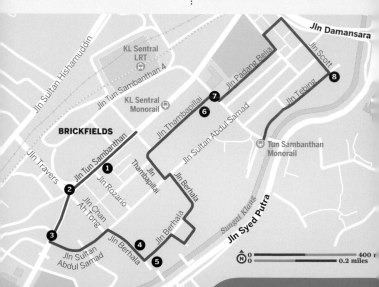

he focal point of KL's official 'Little
ndia'. Symbolic elements in the foun-
ain's design include elephants, swans,
otuses and seven different colours.
The **hawker stalls** (Jln Tun Sambanthan
& Lg Chan Ah Tong; dishes RM5-10; ⏱24hr;
🚈KL Sentral, 🚆KL Sentral) across the road
are great for cheap eats.

③ Garland Sellers

Stroll down lively Jln Tun Sambanthan, passing the decorative arches
and jewellery, sari and video shops
whose competing sound systems
blast out Hindi and Tamil pop music.
Follow the scent of jasmine to find
an alley of **garland stalls** (Jln Tun
Sambanthan; ⏱10am-11pm; 🚈KL Sentral);
pause here to watch the stall holders
skilfully weave the brightly coloured
flowers into garlands used in religious
ceremonies. At the corner with Jln
Sultan Abdul Samad, look for a series
of **murals** depicting the history of
Brickfields.

④ Buddhist Maha Vihara

Enjoy the peaceful surrounds of **Buddhist Maha Vihara** (📞03-2274 1141; www.
buddhistmahavihara.org; 123 Jln Berhala;
🚈KL Sentral, 🚆KL Sentral). Founded in
1894 by Sinhalese settlers, it's one
of KL's major Theravada Buddhist
temples. Meditation classes take place
on Monday and Thursday at 8pm on a
by-donation basis.

⑤ Temple of Fine Arts

Stop for lunch at **Annalakshmi Vegetarian Restaurant** (📞03-2274 0799;
www.facebook.com/AnnalakshmiVegetarian
RestaurantKualaLumpur; 116 Jln Berhala;
dinner mains RM10-18; ⏱11.30am-3pm &
6.30-10pm Tue-Sun; 🍴; 🚈KL Sentral, 🚆KL
Sentral) inside the Temple of Fine Arts,
or you can eat at the humbler **Annalakshmi Riverside** next to the car park
behind the main building, where it's
'eat as you wish, give as you feel'.

**⑥ Sam Kow Tong
Chinese Temple**

Established in 1916 by the Heng Hua
clan, the 'three teachings' **temple** (16
Jln Thambapillai; admission free; ⏱7am-5pm;
KL Sentral) has a beautiful Hokkien-
style temple roof, with graceful curv-
ing ridgelines that taper at the ends
like swallowtails.

⑦ Street Food

Pick up a banana fritter at **Brickfields
Pisang Goreng** (📞012-617 2511; cnr
Jln Thambapillai & Jln Tun Sambanthan 4;
banana fritters RM1.30; ⏱noon-5pm; 🚆Tun
Sambanthan) and wash it down with a
coconut water or *ais cendol* (shaved
ice dessert) from the **ABC stall** across
the road, outside the 7-Eleven.

⑧ Sri Kandaswamy Temple

This **temple** (www.srikandaswamykovil.
org; 3 Lg Scott; admission free; ⏱5.30am-
9pm; 🚆Tun Sambanthan), fronted by an
elaborate modern *gopura* (gateway),
was founded by the Sri Lankan community in 1909 as a place to practise
Shaiva Siddhanta, a major Hindu sect
popular with the diaspora community.

E

MERDEKA SQUARE

Masjid Jamek
LRT

Jln Raja Laut

Sungai Klang

Jln Tun Tan Cheng Lock

Jln Kinabalu

Old KL Train Station

Kuala Lumpur

Jln Sultan Hishamuddin

7

K

D

Masjid Negara
2

Islamic Arts Museum

Jln Kinabalu

Jln Parlimen

Jln Cenderasari

KL Butterfly Park

Jln Lembah Perdana

5

C

Jln Cenderawasih

KL Bird Park
4

Royal Malaysian Police Museum
9

Jln Perdana

Jln Perdana

11

22

LAKE GARDENS

Jln Tembusu

Tun Abdul Razak Heritage Park

Tasik Perdana

B

National Monument
6

Jln Parlimen

Jln Cenderamulia

Jln Cenderamulia

Persiaran Mahameru

Jln Damai

Jln Cenderamulia

Jln Sultan Salahuddin

Tun Abdul Razak Heritage Park

A

1

2

3

4

Jln Istana

Royal Museum 3

Jln Bellamy

Jln Syed Putra

14

Kwong Tong Cemetery 10

24

Jln Scott

15

Jln Tebing

Sungai Klang

Jln Tun Sambanthan 3

26

Jln Tun Sambanthan

Jln Padang Belia

12

Tun Sambanthan Monorail

Tun Sambanthan Monorail

BRICKFIELDS

For reviews see

◉ Top Sights	p94	
◎ Sights	p102	
⊗ Eating	p106	
🅗🅣 Drinking	p109	
🄴 Entertainment	p111	
⑤ Shopping	p111	

400 m
0.2 miles

N

Museum 1 / Jln Sultan...
Orang Asli Craft Museum

Jln Tun Sambanthan 4

16

KL Sentral
LRT

25

21

KL Sentral Monorail

19

Jln Tun Sambanthan

Jln Sultan Abdul Samad

Jln Rozario

Jln Berhala

23

Jln Syed Putra

Bangsar LRT

17

Jln Travers

Jln Travers

Jln Selangor

Lg Travers

Jln Bukit Travers

Jln Bangsar

Jln Kemuja

20

13

27

28

Sights

National Museum

MUSEUM

1 ⊙ Map p100, C5

This museum offers a rich look at Malaysian history, with four galleries covering everything from the formation of the rainforest through to Malaysia today. The best exhibits are Early History, with artefacts from Neolithic and Bronze Age cultures; and the Malay Kingdoms, which highlights the rise of Islamic kingdoms in the Malay Archipelago. Recommended free museum tours are offered at 10am Monday to Saturday and again at 2pm on Thursday. Note that the museum may close for renovations in 2017. (Muzium Negara; ☎ 03-2282 6255; www.muziumnegara.gov. my; Jln Damansara; adult/child RM5/2; ⊙ 9am-6pm; ⏍ KL Sentral)

Local Life

Sri Sakthi Vinayagar Temple

The original **shrine** (Jln Berhala; ⊙ 6am-noon & 5.30-9.30pm; ⏍ Tun Sambanthan) for Lord Vinayagar (the remover of obstacles) in Brickfields was a squatter shack on Jln Sultan Abdul Samad. Such was the humble start of many temples in this immigrant community. It's still rather simple but there is a tender devotional atmosphere to the place, and one statue of Lord Vinayagar inside is made of bananas and brown sugar.

Masjid Negara

MOSQUE

2 ⊙ Map p100, D3

The main place of worship for KL's Malay Muslim population is this gigantic 1960s mosque, inspired by Mecca's Masjid al-Haram. Able to accommodate 15,000 worshippers, it has an umbrella-like blue-tile roof with 18 points symbolising the 13 states of Malaysia and the five pillars of Islam. Rising above the mosque, a 74m-high minaret issues the call to prayer, which can be heard across Chinatown. Non-Muslims are welcome to visit outside prayer times; robes are available for those who are not dressed appropriately. (National Mosque; www. masjidnegara.gov.my; admission free; ⊙ 9am-noon, 3-4pm & 5.30-6.30pm, closed Fri morning; ⏍ Kuala Lumpur)

Royal Museum

MUSEUM

3 ⊙ Map p100, E6

With the 2011 opening of the RM800 million new Istana Negara (National Palace; official residence of Malaysia's head of state) in the city's north, the former palace became the Royal Museum. You can tour the first two floors of the mansion, originally built as a family home in 1928 by Chinese tin tycoon Chan Wing. The palace exterior, with its eclectic European style, looks much the same as it did in Chan Wing's day. To get here, take a taxi from Tun Sambanthan. (Muzium Diraja; www.jmm.gov.my; Jln Istana; adult/child RM10/5; ⊙ 9am-5pm; ⏍ Tun Sambanthan)

Masjid Negara

KL Bird Park
WILDLIFE RESERVE

4 Map p100, C3

This fabulous 21-hectare aviary houses some 3000 birds comprising 200 species of (mostly) Asian birds. The park is divided into four sections: In the first two, birds fly freely beneath an enormous canopy. Section three features the native hornbills (so-called because of their enormous beaks), while section four offers the less-edifying spectacle of caged species. (03-2272 1010; www.klbirdpark.com; Jln Cenderawasih; adult/child RM50/41; 9am-6pm; ; Kuala Lumpur)

KL Butterfly Park
WILDLIFE RESERVE

5 Map p100, C2

This is a great place to get up close with a hundred or so of the 1100-plus butterfly species found in Malaysia, including the enormous and well-named birdwings, the elegant swallowtails, and the colourful tigers and Jezebels. There's also a bug gallery where you can shudder at the size of Malaysia's giant centipedes and spiders. (Taman Rama Rama; 03-2693 4799; www.klbutterflypark.com; Jln Cenderasari; adult/child RM22/11; 9am-6pm; Kuala Lumpur)

Understand

Talking the Talk

- -

As a federation of former British colonies, Malaysia is a fantastic country to visit for English speakers, but linguists will be pleased to tackle the region's multitude of other languages. Malaysia's national language is Bahasa Malaysia. This is often a cause of confusion for travellers, who logically give a literal translation to the two words and refer to the 'Malaysian language'. In fact you cannot speak 'Malaysian'; the language is Malay.

Other languages commonly spoken in the region include Tamil, Hokkien, Cantonese and Mandarin, but there are also Chinese dialects, various other Indian and Orang Asli languages and even, in Melaka, a form of 16th-century Portuguese known as Kristang. All Malaysians speak Malay, and many are fluent in at least two other languages.

Even if you stick to English, you'll have to get used to the local patois – Manglish – which includes plenty of Mandarin, Cantonese and Tamil words and phrases. Many words are used solely to add emphasis and have no formal meaning, which can make things a little confusing. Used incorrectly, Manglish can come across as quite rude, so listen carefully and take local advice before trying it out in polite company. To get you started, here are a few of the most common Manglish words and expressions:

Ah Suffix used for questions, eg 'Why late, ah?'

Got Used for all tenses of the verb 'to have' or in place of 'there is/are', eg 'Got money, ah?' and 'Got noodles in the soup'.

Lah Very common suffix used to affirm statements, eg 'Don't be stupid lah!'

Le Used to soften orders, eg 'Give le'.

Liao Used similarly to 'already', eg 'Finished liao'.

Lor Used for explanations, eg 'Just is lor'.

Meh An expression of skepticism, eg 'Really meh'.

One Adds emphasis to the end of a sentence, eg 'That car so fast one'.

Ready Another form of 'already', eg 'No thanks, eat ready'.

National Monument MONUMENT

6 Map p100, B1

This impressive monument commemorates the defeat of the communists in 1950 and provides fine views across the Tun Abdul Razak Heritage Park and the city. The giant militaristic bronze sculpture was created in 1966 by Felix de Weldon, the artist behind the Iwo Jima monument in Washington, DC, and is framed beautifully by an azure reflecting pool and graceful curved pavilion. (Tugu Negara; Plaza Tugu Negara, Jln Parlimen; admission free; 7am-6pm; Masjid Jamek)

Old KL Train Station HISTORIC BUILDING

7 Map p100, E4

One of KL's most distinctive colonial buildings, this 1910 train station (replaced as a transit hub by KL Sentral in 2001) is a grand if ageing structure designed by British architect AB Hubback in the Mogul (or Indo-Saracenic) style. The building's walls are white plaster, rows of keyhole and horseshoe arches provide ventilation on each level, and large *chatri* and onion domes adorn the roof. (Jln Sultan Hishamuddin; Kuala Lumpur)

Orang Asli Craft Museum MUSEUM

8 Map p100, C5

It's worth dropping into this interesting museum to take a look at the gallery of wood carvings and masks produced by the Mah Meri and Jah Hut peoples. There are also informative displays highlighting the different ethnic groups' origins, traditions and animist beliefs, along with items such as blowpipes used for hunting and a traditional dugout canoe. (03-2282 6255; www.jmm.gov.my; Jln Damansara; adult/child RM5/2; 9am-6pm; KL Sentral)

Royal Malaysian Police Museum MUSEUM

9 Map p100, C4

One of KL's best small museums offers a fascinating history of Malaysia through the story of policing. Discover not just the uniforms that distinguished British- from Dutch- from Sultan-era law enforcers, but also the crime issues that plagued them. The

Top Tip

Between the Gardens & Merdeka Square

The entrance to the Tun Abdul Razak Heritage Park near the Islamic Arts Museum is about 1km from Merdeka Sq. You can easily walk between these two areas along Jln Raja Laut. Another option is to rent a bicycle from **KL By Cycle** (03-2691 1382; www.myhoponhopoff.com; Dataran Merdeka Underground Mall; per hour RM10, deposit RM100; 9am-6pm; Masjid Jamek) at Merdeka Sq.

Top Tip

Lightning Strikes

Malaysia has the world's third-highest incidence of lightning strikes, and deaths sadly do occur. Storms can appear suddenly over KL. It's important to keep an eye on the weather forecast and it's usually best to visit outdoor places such as the Lake Gardens in the morning, when there is less likelihood of a storm. If you see dark clouds or hear thunder, seek shelter in a large building; don't use an umbrella or a mobile phone during a lightning storm.

standout display, though, is the gallery of weapons, from handmade guns and knives, to automatic weapons, to hand grenades and swords, all seized from members of criminal 'secret societies' and communists during the Emergency. (5 Jln Perdana; admission free; ⏰10am-6pm Tue-Sun, closed 12.30-2.30pm Fri; 🚉Kuala Lumpur)

Kwong Tong Cemetery CEMETERY

10 Map p100, E8

This fascinating cemetery lies directly south of the Royal Museum and is notable not just for its immense size (333 hectares of rolling grassy hills and fragrant frangipani trees) but also for the many notables buried within. These include Kapitan Yap Ah Loy, founder of KL. There are also memorials to WWII dead. Pick up a

map at the cemetery office. (www.ktc.org.my; ⏰8.30am-4.30pm; 🚉KL Sentral, 🚇KL Sentral)

Eating

Rebung MALAYSIAN $$

11 Map p100, C2

Occupying the top level of a multistorey car park overlooking the Botanical Gardens, flamboyant celebrity chef Ismail's restaurant Rebung is one of KL's best. The seemingly endless buffet spread is splendid, with all kinds of dishes that you'd typically only be served in a Malay home. Herbs grown on the terrace are used in the recipes. Book ahead at weekends. (📞03-2276 3535; www.restoranrebungdatochefismail.com; 5th fl, 1 Jln Tanglin, Perdana Botanical Garden; buffet lunch/dinner RM42/53; ⏰8am-10pm; ❄️🛜; 🚉Masjid Jamek)

Restoran Yarl SRI LANKAN $$

12 Map p100, D6

This simple restaurant in Brickfields serves tasty Tamil dishes from northern Sri Lanka. Help yourself from clay pots of spicy mutton, chicken and fish *peratal* (dry curry), squid curry, aubergine *sothi* (mild curry with coconut milk) and vegetable dishes. Don't miss the house speciality, crab curry – try a ladle of the sauce if you don't fancy grappling with claws. (www.yarl.com.my; 50 Jln Padang Belia; meals RM10-15; ⏰7am-10pm Tue-Sun; 🚉KL Sentral, 🚇KL Sentral)

Old KL Train Station

Southern Rock Seafood

SEAFOOD $$

13 Map p100, A7

The fishmonger to some of KL's top restaurants has opened its own operation and it's a corker. The fish and seafood – in particular the wide range of oysters – is top quality, simply prepared to allow the flavours to sing. The blue-and-white decor suggests nights spent on the sparkling Med rather than the muddy Sungai Klang. (☏03-2856 2016; www.southernrockseafood.com; 34 Jln Kemuja; mains RM28-65; ☺10am-10pm; ☏; ☐Bank Rakyat-Bangsar)

Ikan Bakar Jalan Bellamy

HAWKER $

14 Map p100, E7

When the king lived nearby it was said he occasionally sent his minions to get an order of grilled stingray from one of the justifiably popular barbecued-fish hawker stalls on the hill behind the former royal palace. There's little to choose between the three of them; wander around and see what takes your fancy. (Jln Bellamy; meals RM10; ☺11am-11pm Mon-Sat; ☐Tun Sambanthan)

Local Life
Brickfields Street Food

Brickfields is the place to go for Indian street food. In a parking lot across the road from KL Sentral, **Ammars** (Asia Parking, Jln Berhala; vadai RM1; ⏰7am-7pm; 🚇KL Sentral, 🚆KL Sentral) is run by a friendly family who fry up tasty snacks, such as lentil *vadai* (fritters) flavoured with fennel seeds, in giant woks. Or head to low-key **Lawanya Food Corner** (📱016-220 2117; 1077/8 Lg Scott; meals RM8; ⏰6am-4pm; 🚆KL Sentral), a simple joint with a few tables lined up under a sheet of corrugated iron, where the same family has been preparing delicious curries for more than 30 years.

Vishal   INDIAN $

15 Map p100, D5

Sit at one of the tables and allow the army of servers to dollop out the great-tasting food on to a banana leaf for you. If you're hungry, supplement the standard meal with a good range of side dishes or a huge mound of chicken biryani. Good for tiffin snacks and a refreshing lassi, too. (📱03-2274 1995; 22 Jln Scott; meals from RM6; ⏰7.30am-10.45pm; 🍴; 🚆Tun Sambanthan)

Jassal Tandoori Restaurant   INDIAN $$

16 Map p100, C6

Jassal serves great-tasting tandoori specialities, what must be the city's best dhal *makhani* (thick dark spicy

lentils), and a load of other dishes including a variety of naans, rotis and *parathas*. Cheap Indian beer is also on offer. At the entrance to the restaurant is **Jesal Sweet House**, a counter selling delicious North Indian sweets. (📱03-2274 6801; 84 Jln Tun Sambanthan; dishes RM17-37; ⏰11am-11pm Mon-Thu, to 11.30pm Fri-Sun; 🚇KL Sentral, 🚆KL Sentral)

Robson Heights Seafood Restaurant   CHINESE $$

17 Map p100, B8

Folks drive from far and wide to feast on the top-class food served at this rickety hillside joint. While its specialities such as stir-fried pig intestines with dried prawn and chilli, braised terrapin, or Marmite crab may not appeal to all, we can vouch for the delicious baked spare ribs in honey sauce and stir-fried udon noodles in black pepper sauce. (📱03-2274 6216; 10b Jln Permai, off Jln Syed Putra; mains RM30-60; ⏰11am-3pm & 5.30-11pm; 🚆Tun Sambanthan)

Colonial Cafe   MALAYSIAN $$$

18 Map p100, D4

British-Malay cuisine, as interpreted by Hainanese chefs of yore, is on the menu at this elegant restaurant in the heritage wing of the Majestic, probably the best spot in KL to feel the privilege and grace of the colonial era. Highlights of the menu include the chicken rice served Melaka style, and the Hainanese chicken chop. (📱03-2785 8000; www.majestickl.com; Majestic Hotel, 5 Jln Sultan

Hishamuddin; mains RM60-170; ⏰noon-2.30pm, 3-6pm & 6.30-11pm; 🚇Kuala Lumpur)

Gem Restaurant INDIAN $$

19 ✘ Map p100, C6

A Brickfields stalwart, this calm, air-conditioned restaurant serves good South Indian food, including specialities from Chettinad, Andhra Pradesh and the Malabar coast. The thali is great value. (☎03-2260 1373; 124 Jln Tun Sambanthan; mains RM10-24; ⏰11.30am-5pm & 6.15-11pm; ❄; 🚇KL Sentral)

Hornbill Restaurant INTERNATIONAL $$

Providing a ringside view of the feathered inhabitants of the KL Bird Park (see 4 ◎ Map p100, C3), this rustic place offers good food without fleecing the tourists too much. Go local with its *nasi lemak* (rice boiled in coconut milk, served with fried anchovies and peanuts) and fried noodles, or please the kids with fish and chips or the homemade chicken or beef burgers. (☎03-2693 8086; www.klbirdpark.com; KL Bird Park, 920 Jln Cenderawasih; mains RM17-30; ⏰9am-7.30pm; 📷; 🚇Kuala Lumpur)

Drinking

Coley COCKTAIL BAR

20 🍸 Map p100, A7

Named after Ada Coleman, a female bartender in 1920s London and creator of the Hanky Panky, this tiny bar at the back of DR.Inc (p111) is the

---

Understand
Drinking in Kuala Lumpur

Like its food scene, KL's drinking options reflect the city's diverse ethnic background. The theatrically served *teh tarik* (literally 'pulled' tea), poured from one pitcher to another to create a frothy brew, can be found at cafes and stalls in the city's Little Indias, while Chinese restaurants invariably serve green tea or pale-yellow chrysanthemum tea, often sweetened with sugar.

Coffee is the chosen fuel of many KLites. Local *kopi* (coffee) is roasted with butter, margarine, rice or sugar, and brewed in a muslin bag; try it sweetened with condensed milk at traditional *kopitiam* (coffee shops). Another unique-to-Malaysia caffeinated drink is *cham* or Hainan tea, a blend of milky coffee and tea. You can also find quality, freshly brewed coffee at a number of hipster cafes in the city.

Despite sky-high alcohol duties, the expertly mixed cocktails on offer at KL's swanky rooftop bars and speakeasy-style cocktail joints are hard to resist. As well as cheap local lagers such as Tiger and Carlsberg, these days you can even find craft beer in KL.

Incense burning, Kwong Tong Cemetery (p106)

place to come for a seriously well-mixed cocktail. Legendary local mixologist CK Kho works the bar, serving a selection of classic cocktails with a contemporary twist. (www.facebook.com/LongLiveColey; 8 Jln Kemuja; ⏰5pm–1am Tue–Sat, 3–9pm Sun; 🚈Bank Rakyat-Bangsar)

Mai Bar
COCKTAIL BAR

21 🚇 Map p100, C6

This Polynesian-style tiki bar, which goes a little too heavy on the red lights, is another addition to KL's growing band of high-rise bars with panoramic city views. DJs spin Wednesday to Saturday after 10pm. For a more casual atmosphere, and

live music Friday nights, try the hotel's W XYZ bar. (www.aloftkualalumpursentral. com; Aloft Kuala Lumpur Sentral, 5 Jln Stesen Sentral; ⏰noon–midnight Sun–Thu, to 2am Fri & Sat; 🛜; 🚉KL Sentral, 🚈KL Sentral)

Kia Klemenz
COFFEE

22 🚇 Map p100, C2

In the small cafe attached to this boutique and gift shop, owner Rokiah prepares coffee from her native Borneo that's worth searching out, as well as a few pastries and snacks. The shop has a good range of handicrafts and textiles such as hand-printed batik and artwork from Sabah. Take a taxi from Masjid Jamek. (www.kiaklemenz.com;

2 Kedai Cenderamata 1, Jln Cenderawasih, Perdana Botanical Garden; ☉9am-6.30pm; 🚇Masjid Jamek)

Entertainment

Temple of Fine Arts THEATRE

23 ⭐ Map p100, C8

Classical Indian dance and music shows take place here throughout the year. The centre also runs performing-arts courses; see the website for schedules. (☎03-2274 3709; www.tfa.org.my; 116 Jln Berhala; ☉closed Mon; 🚇KL Sentral, 🚈KL Sentral)

Shopping

DR.Inc HOMEWARES

Lisette Scheers is the creative force behind the Nala brand of homeware, stationery, accessories and other arty items. All her products embody a contemporary but distinctly local design aesthetic and are beautifully displayed at this Instagram dream of a concept shop and cafe (see 20 ☕ Map p100, A7). (☎03-2283 4698; www.facebook.com/thincacademykl; 8 Jln Kemuja; ☉9am-7pm; 🛜; 🚇Bank Rakyat-Bangsar)

Lavanya Arts ARTS & CRAFTS

Lavanya, inside the Temple of Fine Arts (see 23 ⭐ Map p110, C8), sells colourful craft goods including adorable kids' and adults' clothes and home decorations. Come the week around

Deepavali for a festive range of beautiful Indian tribal arts, as well as handsome painted wooden dolls, brass sculpture, and colourful furniture from Rajasthan. (www.facebook.com/lavanyaarts; Temple of Fine Arts, 114-116 Jln Berhala; ☉10am-9.30pm Tue-Sat, to 3pm Sun; 🚇KL Sentral)

Sonali FASHION & ACCESSORIES

24 🔒 Map p100, E6

Sequins, silks, filigree patterns and tie-dye – all the elements of the flash Bollywood look are present in this boutique. It's mainly for women but also has some fancy tops for men. (www.sonali.com.my; 67a Jln Scott; ☉10am-7pm Mon-Sat; 🚈Tun Sambanthan)

Nu Sentral MALL

25 🔒 Map p100, C6

Providing the connection between the monorail and the main station at KL Sentral is this shiny, multilevel mall. Among many shops there's a branch

---

⭕ Local Life
Tugu Drum Circle

A great way to try something different and meet friendly locals is to join the **Tugu Drum Circle** (☉5.30-8.30pm Sun; 🚇Masjid Jamek), an open group for drummers that meets at Plaza Tugu Negara in the Tun Abdul Razak Heritage Park on Sundays from 5.30pm till 8.30pm. Beginners are welcome. See their Facebook page for details.

Understand

Literature

A 1911 scandal involving the wife of a headmaster at a KL school who was convicted in a murder trial after shooting dead a male friend was the basis for Somerset Maugham's short story and play *The Letter*. Anthony Burgess picked up the thread of the dying days of British colonial rule in the region in *The Malayan Trilogy*, written in the 1950s when he was a school teacher in the country; it was Burgess who coined the phrase 'cooler lumpur'. *The Malayan Life of Ferdach O'Haney* is a fictionalised account of author Frederick Lees' experiences in 1950s Malaya; Lees was uniquely placed to observe mid-20th-century life in KL in his role as a top-ranking civil servant.

The literary baton has long since been passed to locally born writers such as Tash Aw (www.tash-aw.com), whose debut novel, *The Harmony Silk Factory*, won the 2005 Whitbread First Novel Award; Man Booker Prize–nominated author Tan Twan Eng (www.tantwaneng.com), whose literature fuses a fascination with Malaysia's past and an exploration of the impact of Japanese culture; and Preeta Samarasan (www.preetasamarasan.com), whose novel *Evening Is the Whole Day* shines a light on the experiences of an Indian immigrant family in the early 1980s.

Samarasan is one of the writers whose work features in *Urban Odysseys*, edited by Janet Tay and Eric Forbes, a mixed bag of short stories set in KL. An excellent collection of locally penned short stories about different aspects of sexuality is *Body 2 Body*, edited by Jerome Kugan and Pang Khee Teik. This anthology has a story by Brian Gomez, whose comedy-thriller *Devil's Place* is fun to read and very evocative of its KL setting. Kam Raslan's *Confessions of an Old Boy* is another comic tale, this time following the adventures both at home and abroad of politico Dato' Hamid.

A snappy read is Amir Muhammad's *Rojak: Bite-Sized Stories*, in which the multi-talented artist and writer gathers a selection of the 350-word vignettes, many of them comic, that he penned as part of the British Council–sponsored creative-writing project City of Shared Stories.

of Parkson department store, a MPH bookshop, a GSC multiplex and a food court, as well as the escape game complex Breakout (www.breakout.com.my). (www.nusentral.com; 201 Jln Tun Sambanthan; ⏱10am-10pm; 🚇KL Sentral, 🚆KL Sentral)

Wei-Ling Gallery ART

26 🔒 Map p100, D5

The top two floors of this old shophouse have been imaginatively turned into a contemporary gallery to showcase local artists. Note the artwork covering the metal security gate in front of the shophouse next door. (www.weiling-gallery.com; 8 Jln Scott; ⏱10am-6pm Mon, 11am-7pm Tue-Fri, 10am-5pm Sat, by appointment only Sun; 🚇KL Sentral, 🚆KL Sentral)

Comoddity CLOTHING

27 🔒 Map p100, A8

Up-and-coming Malaysian menswear designer Vincent Siow has shown at KL fashion week as well as at street shows in Paris and Shanghai. His label Comoddity specialises in unique

GOKL City Bus

The Tun Abdul Razak Heritage Park is huge, and in KL's heat and humidity getting to and from the sights can be a slog. The free GOKL City Bus red line links KL Sentral with Masjid Negara, the National Museum and Merdeka Sq.

pieces such as hand-painted trousers, suit jackets adorned with cityscape motifs and purple PVC bomber jackets. The boutique also acts as a gallery for Siow's artwork. (www.thecomoddity.com; upper ground fl, Bangsar Village II, cnr Jln Telawi 1 & Jln Telawi 2; ⏱10am-10pm; 🚇Bank Rakyat-Bangsar)

d.d.collective FASHION & ACCESSORIES

28 🔒 Map p100, A8

Contemporary, high-end fashion for men and women by Paris-based Malaysian designer Jonathan Liang. (dd-collective.com; Bangsar Village II, cnr Jln Telawi 1 & Jln Telawi 2; ⏱10am-10pm; 🚇Bank Rakyat-Bangsar)

Top Sights
Thean Hou Temple

Getting There

🚊Tun Sambanthan, then taxi.

Sitting atop Robson Heights, this imposing, multi-layered Chinese temple is one of the most visually impressive in Malaysia. Dedicated to the heavenly mother, Thean Hou, it provides wonderful views of KL and is a great place to visit on a Buddhist festival such as Wesak Day or during Chinese New Year.

History & Design

The temple was officially opened in 1989 and cost the Selangor and Federal Territory Hainan Association RM7 million to build. You can see pretty much every ringgit in its rich architectural detail which includes decorative balustrades, beams, eaves, murals, and flying dragons and phoenixes. Arranged on four levels, the temple is fronted by a **statue of Thean Hou** beside a wishing well and a garden studded with large statues of the **signs of the Chinese zodiac**. On the ground floor there are souvenir stalls, a canteen and a marriage registration office – this is a very popular spot for weddings. The 1st floor has a large hall where religious and cultural events are held while the 2nd has the temple's administrative offices.

Main Prayer Hall

Thean Hou's statue takes centre stage in the main hall on the 3rd floor with Kuan Yin (the Buddhist goddess of mercy) on her right and Shuiwei Shengniang (goddess of the waterfront) to her left. Smaller statues of Milefo (the laughing Buddha), Weituo and Guandi contribute to this Taoist–Buddhist hotchpotch. Climb to the terrace above for wonderful views and then go back down behind the temple past a medicinal herb garden and a pond packed with tortoises.

Fortune Sticks

In the main prayer hall, look for the fortune-telling sticks: pick up the bunch of sticks, then drop them back in their jar so that one sticks up the tallest. The number on it will correspond to a drawer containing a slip of paper with your fortune on it.

📞 03-2274 7088

www.hainannet.com.my/en

off Jln Syed Putra

admission free

🕐 8am-10pm

☑ Top Tips

▶ Go up to the rooftop terrace for views across the city to the Menara KL and Petronas Towers. It's a great spot for photos or watching the sun set.

▶ Come early in the morning for a peaceful visit before the tour buses arrive.

✗ Take a Break

The **canteen** (dishes RM5-10; 🕐 8am-10pm) on the ground floor of the temple serves simple Chinese dishes.

For a more extravagant meal, head to Robson Heights Seafood Restaurant (p108).

Local Life
Boutique-Hopping in Bangsar Baru

This former rubber plantation district turned wealthy suburb is where new trends in shopping and eating come to live (and then die before they lose their edge). In a few compact blocks you'll find terraced restaurants and specialty cafes, artisanal bakeries luring passers-by with the aroma of fresh bread, plus aspiring local designers and two high-end malls.

Getting There

Bangsar Baru is east of Brickfields.

🚕 A taxi from downtown is easiest.

🚌 Bangsar then taxi.

❶ Thisappear

This gallery-like **space** (☎03-2201 2290; www.thisappearplus.com; 1st fl, 51 Jln Telawi 3; ☺noon-8pm) that's co-owned by four young designers is a great place to check out some of Malaysia's best up-and-coming designers including Joe Chia, Kozo, Justin Chew and Alia Bastaman.

❷ I Love Snackfood

Stop by this quirky **boutique** (☎03-2201 7513; www.ilovesnackfood.com; 17a Jln Telawi 3; ☺11am-7pm) specialising in kitsch interior decor to browse the typewriters, globes and gorgeous stationery.

❸ Jaslyn Cakes

If you need a snack, head to this tiny **bakery** (☎03-2202 2868; www.jaslyncakes. com; 7a Jln Telawi 2; cakes per portion RM3-10; ☺11am-7pm Tue-Fri, to 8pm Sat & Sun; 🚇Bank Rakyat-Bangsar) that's justifiably popular for its exquisite cakes, pastries, breads and biscuits. For something savoury, go for a banana-leaf meal at banana-leaf meal seller **Sri Nirwana Maju** (☎03-2287 8445; 43 Jln Telawi 3; meals RM5-16; ☺10am-2am).

❹ Never Follow Suit

This vintage and original design **boutique** (www.facebook.com/Never.Follow. Suit.Bangsar; 28-2, Jln Telawi 2; ☺11am-9pm) is a good first stop for the fashion-conscious. Also look for **Shoes Shoes Shoes** (www.shoesshoesshoes.com.my; 22 Jln Telawi 3; ☺11am-9pm) and **Mimpikita** (www.mimpikita.com.my; 1st fl, 15 Jln Telawi 2; ☺11am-7pm Mon-Sat) for high-end local fashion made with gorgeous printed fabrics, as well as jewellery by Dipped Row.

❺ Bangsar Village I & II

These twin **malls** (www.bangsarvillage. com; cnr Jln Telawi 1 & Jln Telawi 2; ☺10am-10pm) are linked by a covered bridge and house upmarket crafts and fashions. Look for local designers including Jonathan Liang at d.d.collective, Comoddity menswear by Vincent Siow and TriBeCa for children's clothing and accessories. Pick up a tome at the local bookshop and publisher Silver-fish Books.

❻ Relax at Hammam Spa

This mosaic-tiled Moroccan **spa** (☎03-2282 2180; www.hammamspas.com; treatments RM116-398; ☺10am-10.30pm) is located on the 3rd floor of Bangsar Village II. Couples and singles packages are available with titles such as the Royal Couple (RM730) and the Sultan's Daughter Wedding (RM456).

❼ Sundowners at Mantra Bar

Head to **Mantra Bar** (www.mantrabarkl. com; ☺4.30pm-1.30am Sun & Tue-Thu, to 3am Fri & Sat) on the rooftop of Bangsar Village II for a happy-hour cocktail (from 4.30pm to 7pm) with views of the KL skyline. Nearby, **Ril's Bar** (☎03-2201 3846; www.rils.com.my; 30 Jln Telawi 5; ☺6pm-1am Sun-Thu, to 3am Fri & Sat; 🛜) has a prohibition-era style cocktail bar upstairs.

The Best of
Kuala Lumpur

Flamingos, KL Bird Park (p103)
ZHUKOVA VALENTYNA / SHUTTERSTOCK ©

Best Walks
Chinatown Architecture

🏃 The Walk

The focus of this walk is the variety of architecture found in the oldest part of town: from eclectic two- and three-storey shophouses to Cantonese-style temples, Dravidian-style Hindu temples, art deco buildings and a Mughal-style mosque. There are endless places to snack, and as much of the walk is covered you can do this any time of day in comfort.

Start Masjid Jamek LRT Station

Finish Petaling Street Market

Length 1.5km; 1½ hours

🍴 Take a Break

Stop for a local breakfast of Hainanese coffee, soft-boiled eggs and *kaya* toast at **Cafe Old Market Square** (p67).

❶ Masjid Jamek

From the station head south down the new river embankment path running parallel to Jln Benteng; look back for a great view of Mughal-inspired **Masjid Jamek** (p60) with its newly uncovered steps down to the river.

❷ Medan Pasar

At the junction with Lr Ampang is **Medan Pasar** (p62), site of KL's original market square. In the southwestern corner of the square, stop to look at **Cafe Old Market Square**. Note the fine Dutch gables, yellow shutters and glassless windows.

❸ OCBC Building

Where Medan Pasar meets Lr Pasar Besar you'll see the **OCBC Building**, a graceful art deco structure built in 1938 for the Overseas Chinese Banking Company. Around the corner with Jln Tun HS Lee is **MS Ally Company**, a pharmacy in business since 1909.

SHAIFULZAMRI / SHUTTERSTOCK ©

Guandi Temple

❹ Sin Sze Si Ya Temple

Cross Lr Pudu, turn right and, after 25m, duck left into an alley leading to the atmospheric **Sin Sze Si Ya Temple** (p60).

❺ Central Market

Exit the way you came in, cross the street and walk two blocks up to the **Central Market** (p61), one of KL's most handsome art deco buildings.

❻ Lee Rubber Building

Exit the market on to Jln Hang Kasturi, then turn left on to Jln Hang Lekir, then right on to Jln Tun HS Lee. The shophouses along here are among Chinatown's oldest. On the south corner is the pale-yellow-painted art deco **Lee Rubber Building**.

❼ Guandi Temple

Opposite, next to the bright-red, incense-wreathed **Guandi Temple** (p61), is Jln Sang Guna, a covered arcade housing Chinatown's atmospheric wet market.

❽ Sri Mahamariamman Temple

Back on Jln Tun HS Lee pause to admire the **Sri Mahamariamman Temple** (p56) and breathe in the sweet jasmine of the flower sellers outside.

❾ Petaling Street Market

At the junction with Jln Sultan turn left, then left on to Jln Petaling, where you can browse **Petaling Street Market** (p70).

Best Walks
A Stroll Through Kampung Baru

🏃 The Walk

Beyond the city's blockbuster sights, this walk offers a fascinating tour of the village side of KL, passing traditional wood houses on stilts, the religious buildings and shrines of multiple faiths, and great places to snack on local dishes. There's not much shade on this walk so start early or head out after 4pm. Dress conservatively (a scarf to cover the head is recommended for women) as you will be entering a mosque and Sikh temple.

Start Chow Kit monorail station

Finish Dang Wangi LRT station

Length 3.5km; two hours

🍴 Take a Break

At the start of the walk there are stalls inside Bazaar Baru Chow Kit, including **Murtabak Ana** (p84). Otherwise, halfway through the tour, stop at **Kak Som** (p84).

❶ Bazaar Baru Chow Kit

From Chow Kit station, walk south along Jln TAR and cross over to the entrance to **Bazaar Baru Chow Kit** (p84). Explore the market's shaded alleys and hangars, pausing for a snack or a drink along the way.

❷ Tatt Khalsa Diwan Gurdwara

Emerge, blinking into the bright light, on Jln Raja Alang, heading east to the Sikh temple **Tatt Khalsa Diwan Gurdwara** (p80). Visitors are welcome to go inside to see the prayer hall or stop for a free cup of tea or simple meal in the canteen.

❸ Masjid Jamek Kampung Baru

Further along is **Masjid Jamek Kampung Baru** (p82), the area's principal mosque.

❹ Viewpoint

Where Jln Raja Alang turns south, continue on the smaller road ahead to the end where you'll turn right at a two-level apartment block: **two palms** in a small field

Durian stall, Bazaar Baru Chow Kit

WILAYAH PERSEKUTUAN / SHUTTERSTOCK ©

perfectly frame the Petronas Towers.

5 Rumah Limas

At the junction of Jln Raja Muda Musa and Jln Raja Mahadi stands a photogenic **turquoise-and-white painted house** dating from 1913; explore Jln Raja Mahadi and the cross streets to see more such traditional wooden houses.

6 Sultan Sulaiman Club

Cross Jln Raja Abdullah to Jln Datuk Abdul Razak. At the end of a playing field is the handsome black-and-white painted reconstruction of the original **Sultan Sulaiman Club.**

7 Master Mat's House

Continue west along Jln Datuk Abdul Razak, stopping at the corner to look at **Master Mat's house**, a handsome blue home built in 1921 by a former school headmaster. Look for the coconut trees in the garden; the family planted one for each child. Turn left and continue past the new **Sultan Sulaiman Club** (p80) building.

8 Dang Wangi Houses

South along Jln Raja Abdullah, off to the left, you'll pass more wooden homes as the concrete city starts to resume. Just before the end of this walk, at the footbridge across to Dang Wangi LRT station, look carefully for one more **wooden yellow house**.

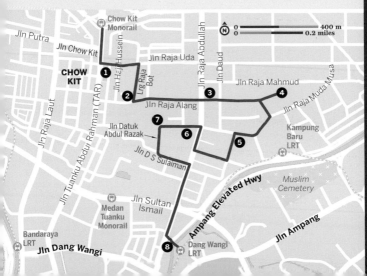

Best
Street Food &
Food Courts

KL's tastiest and best-value food is found at hawker stalls, and locals are fiercely loyal to their favourite vendors. Many hawkers have been in business for decades or operate a business inherited from their parents or even their grandparents; the best enjoy reputations that exceed their geographical reach.

The Hawker Scene

To sample Malaysian hawker food, simply head to a stand-alone streetside kitchen-on-wheels, a *kopitiam* (coffee shop) or food court. Food courts sometimes have a mix of Indian, Malay and Chinese dishes, but often one ethnic cuisine will be featured.

Intrepid eaters shouldn't overlook *pasar* (markets). Morning markets include stalls selling coffee and other beverages, as well as vendors preparing foods such as freshly griddled roti and curry and *chee cheong fun* (rice noodle roll). *Pasar malam* (night markets) are also excellent places to graze.

There's little to fear about eating from outdoor hawker stalls or food markets, but if you want some air-conditioning and a little more comfort, there's no shortage of indoor food courts in KL's malls.

Ordering

Place your order with one or multiple vendors, find a seat (shared tables are common) and pay for each dish as it's delivered to your table. You'll be approached by someone taking drink orders after you've sat down – pay for these separately as well.

☑ Top Tip

▶ If you're intrigued by the food you've sampled in KL and feel you want a bit of expert guidance to help you learn and sample more, consider a food tour with **Simply Enak** (☎ 017-287 8929; www. simplyenak.com; tours RM200-250).

Best Hawker Food

Little India Fountain Hawker Stalls Collection of stalls for roti or banana-leaf meals. (p98)

Keong Kee Sit under a tree with a coconut curry or wild-boar curry. (p51)

Jalan Alor KL's most famous food street, with dozens of choices. (p40)

Left: Banana-leaf meal; Above: Jalan Alor

Kin Kin Much-loved purveyor of chilli *pan mee* (p82)

Best Food Courts

Lot 10 Hutong Enjoy famous hawker food in an air-conditioned food court. (p29)

Food Republic Excellent choice of meals and snacks at the Pavilion KL mall. (p36)

Best Market Food

Bazaar Baru Chow Kit Sample noodles in a rich cow's-liver soup and an array of Malay desserts. (p84)

Masjid India Pasar Malam A wide range of excellent food stalls at this Saturday-night market. (p84)

Best Kopitiam

Yut Kee Old-school joint serving Hainanese comfort dishes such as chicken chops. (p83)

Capital Cafe Beloved multi-hawker venue for Malay and Chinese dishes. (p84)

Hong Ngek This long-running joint serves excellent ginger duck and ribs in Guinness. (p67)

Best Local Breakfast

Imbi Market at ICC Pudu Try the *popiah*, congee and egg tarts. (p51)

Chee Cheong Fun Stall Best rice noodles in Chinatown. (p66)

Worth a Trip

Off the tourist radar but renowned locally, **Glutton Street** (Pudu Wai Sek Kai; Jln Sayur; noodles RM5-10; ⏰most stalls 5pm-midnight; 🚇Pudu), a hawker stall alley near Pudu Market, comes to life at night. Evening grazing could include addictive fried chicken, *chai tow kway* (radish cake stir-fried with soy sauce, bean sprouts and egg), prawn fritters and barbecued dried squid, all for bargain prices.

Best
Bars & Cafes

Bubble tea, iced *kopi-o*, a frosty beer or a flaming Lamborghini – KL's cafes, teahouses and bars offer a multitude of ways to wet your whistle. Muslim mores push coffee and tea culture to the fore, but there's no shortage of sophisticated cocktail bars and other alcohol-fuelled venues where you can party the night away with abandon.

Bars

Sky-high duties on alcohol can make a boozy night out awfully expensive, but KL sort of makes up for that by offering such fabulous city views from its many elevated venues. The cheapest beers are those brewed locally, such as Tiger and Carlsberg; they're best enjoyed alfresco while watching the streetside theatre of Jln Alor or Chinatown's Jln Hang Lekir. KLites are also partial to an expertly mixed cocktail, which can be sampled at one of the city's many rooftop bars or one of the growing number of speakeasy-style 'secret' bars.

Cafes

Traditional Malaysian *kopi* is popular in KL's *kopitiam* (coffee shops). This dark, bitter brew is served in Chinese coffee shops and is an excellent antidote to a case of jet lag.

There's no need to go without your daily dose of latte or espresso, though. The traditional *kopitiam* and their contemporary counterparts are rivalled by a host of excellent independent cafes that deal in single-origin beans and employ baristas trained to use classic coffee-making machines.

☑ Top Tip

▶ Upscale bars and clubs usually have a dress code. Don't turn up in flip-flops and shorts.

Best Cocktail Bars

Omakase + Appreciate Speakeasy joint on the edge of Chinatown. (p68)

PS150 Shanghai-style drinking den concealed behind a fake toy shop. (p68)

Coley Tiny cocktail bar serving expertly mixed drinks. (p109)

Ril's Bar Sophisticated assignation spot with inventive mixologists. (p117)

Left: *Kopi;* Above: Heli Lounge Bar

Best Sky Bars

Heli Lounge Bar Thrilling rooftop drinks in the heart of Bukit Bintang. (p40)

Marini's on 57 Book a seat for a bird's-eye view of KLCC. (p41)

Mantra Bar KL Look across the suburbs to the KL skyline from the rooftop of Bangsar Village mall. (p117)

Mai Bar Fun poolside bar overlooking KL Sentral. (p110)

Best Cafes & Teahouses

VCR Latte-art-contest-winning baristas serve up quality brews. (p51)

Feeka Coffee Roasters Choose from microlot beans or espresso-based drinks. (p41)

TWG Tea Classy tea emporium in Pavilion KL. (p42)

Chocha Foodstore Sample the hot and cold blends selected by the in-house 'tea sommelier'. (p69)

Best LGBT Friendly

DivineBliss Saturday-night rooftop party with renowned guest DJs. (p44)

Marketplace Sweat it out on the dance floor, cool off on the roof. (p44)

Moontree House Come here to tap into KL's discreet lesbian scene. (p69)

Worth a Trip

The city's newest entertainment complex, **TREC** (436 Jln Tun Razak; AirAsia-Bukit Bintang), is located a taxi ride east of Bukit Bintang on Jln Tun Razak. Catch some stand-up comedy at Live House (p45) or head to the superclub **Zouk** (www.zoukclub.com.my).

Best
Shopping

Kuala Lumpur is a prize fighter on the Asian shopping parade, a serious rival to retail heavyweights Singapore, Bangkok and Hong Kong. On offer are appealing handicrafts, major international brands (both legit and fake versions), masses of malls and decent sale prices. The city's traditional markets are hugely enjoyable and atmospheric experiences, regardless of whether you have a purchase in mind.

What to Buy

Skilled artisans may be a dying breed, but you can still find great handmade craft items for sale in KL. Fashion, contemporary-art galleries, antique stores and interior-design shops are also worth a look.

Textiles

Batik is produced by drawing or printing a pattern on fabric with wax, then dyeing the material. The wax contains the various colours and, when washed away, leaves the pattern. Batik can be made into clothes or homewares or simply displayed as works of art.

Another textile to look out for is *kain songket,* a luxurious fabric with gold and silver threads woven throughout the material.

Basketry & Mengkuang

All sorts of useful household items are made using rattan, bamboo, swamp nipah grass and pandanus leaves. Mengkuang (a local form of weaving) uses pandanus leaves and strips of bamboo to make baskets, bags and mats. Look in the Central Market and around Chinatown for these items.

Best Malls

Pavilion KL Setting the gold standard for Bukit Bintang's malls. (p46)

Suria KLCC A retail nirvana at the base of the Petronas Towers. (p47)

Publika Spend a day browsing the shops, the galleries and the many great places to eat. (p48)

Best for Local Handicrafts

Asli Craft Beautiful items handmade by indigenous groups from across Malaysia. (p70)

Wau Tradisi Traditional paper and bamboo kites. (p73)

Rhino Hand-painted clogs and other handicrafts. (p71)

Left: *Kain songket*; Above: Royal Selangor Visitor Centre

Best Museum Shops

Islamic Arts Museum
Top-notch range of arts and crafts and design and art books. (p96)

Gahara Galleria The National Textiles Museum shop sells quality batik and local designer goods. (p70)

Museum of Ethnic Arts Nearly everything is for sale at this extraordinary private collection of local tribal arts. (p70)

Kompleks Kraf The Karakenya section is stacked with all kinds of batik prints. (p34)

Best for Fashion

Khoon Hooi Luxury fashion with an edge from an award-winning designer. (p47)

Comoddity Original pieces by local menswear designer Vincent Siow. (p113)

d.d.collective Contemporary high-end fashion by Paris-based Malaysian designer Jonathan Liang. (p113)

Mimpikita Local fashion made with gorgeous printed fabrics. (p117)

Aseana Plenty of bling-tastic frocks, including pieces by top designer Nurita Harith. (p49)

Worth a Trip

Located 8km northeast of the city centre, the **Royal Selangor Visitor Centre** (☎ 03-4145 6122; www.royalselangor. com/visitor-centre; 4 Jln Usahawan 6, Setapak Jaya; ⏰ 9am-5pm; 🚇 Wangsa Maju) offers some very appealing pewter souvenirs. Also for sale are the company's silver pieces under the Comyns brand and its Selberam jewellery. You can tour the factory and try your hand at creating a pewter dish or jewellery. Get a taxi from Wangsa Maju station.

Best
With Kids

KL has a lot going for it as a family-holiday destination. Its textbook Southeast Asian cultural mix offers chances to watch temple ceremonies and sample an amazing range of food. Nature is also close at hand, along with clean accommodation, modern malls and fun amusement parks.

Eating Out

KL's myriad dining outlets offer meals that will appeal to the fussiest of kids. Although you may not think it, a busy food stall is usually the safest place to eat – you can see the food being prepared, the ingredients are often fresh and if the wok stays hot there's little chance of bacteria. Grown-ups can also try adventurous dishes while the kids get something more familiar.

Best Attractions for Kids

Batu Caves The colourful tableaux of Hindu myths, wild monkeys and the Dark Caves capture children's imagination. (p88)

Aquaria KLCC In the heart of KL, kids can interact with sea creatures. (p34)

KL Bird Park This massive free-flight aviary filled with exotic birds is a family highlight. (p103)

Menara Kuala Lumpur Take a jungle walk before or after a ride up this telecommunications tower. (p26)

Petrosains A good hands-on science centre for kids. (p36)

Avenue K Don't miss the interactive dinosaur exhibition, Discoveria. (p49)

Petronas Towers View the city from on high and learn about the construction of the iconic buildings. (p24)

☑ Top Tips

▶ **Time Out KL** (www.timeout.com/kuala-lumpur/kids) publishes a *Malaysia for Kids* guide and its website has up-to-date listings and features on what to do with your kids.

▶ Malaysian drinks are very sweet and even fresh juices usually have sugar added. To cut down on sugar, ask for drinks without sugar or order bottled water.

Thean Hou Temple The colourful temple offers photo ops of Chinese zodiac statues, flying dragons and a pool teeming with tortoises. (p115)

Best
For Free

Much of the best of KL is completely free for visitors. This includes all temples and mosques, public parks, some museums, and many architecturally interesting buildings, such as Chinatown shophouses. People-watching along busy streets and in markets are also fun activities that don't break the bank, and Visit KL offers free tours of Merdeka Sq and Kampung Baru.

Best Free Museums & Galleries

ILHAM Slick gallery showcasing modern and contemporary Malaysian art. (p32)

Bank Negara Malaysia Museum & Art Gallery Surprisingly interesting exhibits on money, including rare coins. (p78)

National Textiles Museum Displays a range of gorgeous examples of local textiles. (p62)

Royal Malaysian Police Museum Fascinating museum charting Malaysia's history of policing. (p105)

Museum of Ethnic Arts Splendid private collection of arts and crafts from Malaysia and abroad. (p70)

Galeri Petronas Swap consumerism for culture at this excellent art gallery showcasing contemporary photography and paintings. (p33)

Best Free Parks & Gardens

KLCC Park Beautiful trees and views of the Twin Towers. (p25)

KL Forest Eco Park A real jungle right in the heart of the city. (p27)

Perdana Botanical Garden Explore exotic native and foreign plants and then stroll around the lake. (p95)

Best Free Places of Worship

Sri Mahamariamman Temple This temple is always a buzzing hive of religious activity. (p56)

Sin Sze Si Ya Temple KL's oldest Chinese temple has a deep devotional atmosphere. (p60)

Masjid Jamek A centre of worship and a beautiful building in the Indo-Saracenic style. (p60)

Batu Caves The main cave of this Hindu shrine is free. (p88)

Guandi Temple Atmospheric temple dedicated to Guandi. (p61)

Best Free Historic Site

Merdeka Square Malaysia's independence square is surrounded by handsome colonial architecture. (p54)

Best
Clubs &
Entertainment

KL has plenty of entertainment options, but you have to keep your ear to the ground to discover the best of what's going on. Conservative tastes and censorship mean that quite a lot of what is on offer is bland and inoffensive, but occasionally controversial and boundary-pushing performances and events are staged.

Theatre & Concerts

Major international popular-music artists often add KL to their Asia tours, but they sometimes have to adapt their shows to accommodate devout Muslim sensibilities.

If you want to see and hear traditional Malaysian dance and music, there are regular shows at the **Malaysia Tourism Centre** (MaTiC; ☏ 03-9235 4900; www.matic.gov.my/en; 109 Jln Ampang; ⏰ 8am-10pm; 🚇 Bukit Nanas) during the day, as well as every night at the nearby restaurant **Saloma** (☏ 03-2161 0122; www.saloma.com.my; 139 Jln Ampang; show only RM60, buffet & show RM100; ⏰ show 8.30-9.30pm, buffet 7-10pm; 🚇 Bukit Nanas). The Central Market's Kasturi Walk is the stage for free music and dance events at the weekends. The beautifully renovated Panggung Bandaraya theatre is the venue for Mud (p69), a light-hearted musical telling the story of KL.

Various restaurants and bars, including Pisco Bar (p41), have live music, and Live House (p127) at the new entertainment complex TREC hosts regular live comedy and music. Jazz is also popular (check out the lineup at No Black Tie, p43), and the accomplished Malaysian Philharmonic Orchestra is well worth catching in concert at the Dewan Filharmonik Petronas (p44).

Best Live Music

No Black Tie Intimate space hosting jazz and classical-music concerts. (p43)

Dewan Filharmonik Petronas Gorgeous classical concert hall at the foot of the Petronas Towers. (p44)

Live House Comedy and live music at the new entertainment complex TREC. (p45)

KL Live Large venue for rock and pop concerts. (p44)

Left: Istana Budaya (p86); Above: Panggung Bandaraya theatre

Best Clubs

Zouk Multizoned dance space that keeps on pumping till 5am. (p127)

Zion Club Stumble home in the early hours from this club on Changkat Bukit Bintang. (p43)

Nagaba Come for the rooftop mojito bar and the 2nd-floor club. (p42)

Best for Movies

GSC Pavilion KL Treat yourself to the Gold Class section. (p45)

TGV Cineplex Get your Hollywood fix at this multiplex. (p45)

Coliseum Theatre Go Bollywood at this historic Masjid India theatre. (p86)

Worth a Trip

Part of the Sentul West regeneration project, the **Kuala Lumpur Performing Arts Centre** (KLPAC; ☎03-4047 9000; www.klpac.org; Sentul Park, Jln Strachan; ⌕Sentul) puts on a wide range of progressive theatrical events including dramas, musicals and dance. Also on offer are performing arts courses and screenings of art-house movies. Combine a show with a stroll in the peaceful leafy grounds and dinner. Sentul Park is 2.5km west of Titiwangsa.

Best
Religious &
Heritage Buildings

KL was first forged by the labours of Chinese, Indians and Malays, all very religiously oriented peoples who, not surprisingly, have left the city with a splendid legacy of temples and mosques. The fourth major part in the city's development, the British, bequeathed a colonial architectural heritage that runs from Tudor-style clubhouses to grand railway stations inspired by the Mughal empire in India.

Best Religious Sites

Masjid Negara The National Mosque is a classic piece of modern architecture. (p102)

Temple Cave A 40m statue of Lord Murugan guards the entrance to the Hindu shrine at Batu Caves. (p89)

Sri Mahamariamman Temple Venerable Hindu shrine in Chinatown. (p56)

Masjid Jamek Recently restored mosque sporting elegant Mogul-influenced design. (p60)

Sin Sze Si Ya Temple Atmospheric Chinese temple dedicated to one of KL's founding fathers. (p60)

Thean Hou Temple Fabulous Buddhist temple on a leafy hill overlooking the city. (p115)

Buddhist Maha Vihara Historic Sinhalese Buddhist temple in Brickfields. (p99)

Best Heritage Buildings

Sultan Abdul Samad Building Glorious brick structure with Moorish architectural influences and 43m clock tower. (p55)

Old KL Train Station A Mogul fantasy, once the rail hub of the peninsula. (p105)

Stadium Merdeka Sporting venue where independence of the Federation of Malaya was declared in 1957. (p64)

Sultan Sulaiman Club City's oldest Malay club, in the heart of Kampung Baru. (p80)

Rumah Penghulu Abu Seman Traditional wooden stilt house from Kedah in the grounds of Badan Warisan Malaysia. (p33)

Loke Chow Kit Mansion Visit KL's new office is in the beautifully restored building once owned by the tin-mining magnate. (p146)

Best
Green Spaces

One of the pleasures of riding around KL in a taxi is suddenly coming round a bend into a stretch of intense greenery, often with towering banyan trees interweaving overhead that block out the sky. There are few small parks to relax in, but plenty of tree-lined roads and a number of larger lakes and forest parks both within the city and a short drive away.

Wild Kuala Lumpur

Even in the city your chances of spotting exotic wildlife are high. Macaque monkeys are out in force at Batu Caves (do not touch or feed them, or other wildlife, as rabies is present in Malaysia). At FRIM also look for adorable dusky leaf monkeys. If you have a vantage over the forest canopy, keep an eye out for brightly coloured orioles and bee-eaters. Anytime you are near a body of water watch for monitor lizards, which can reach up to 2m in length.

Best Parks & Lakes

KLCC Park Jogging track, great kids' playground, top views of Petronas Towers. (p25)

Titiwangsa Lake Gardens Serene park surrounding a large lake in northern KL. (p78)

KL Forest Eco Park
Traverse the canopy walkway in this lowland dipterocarp forest in the heart of the city. (p27)

Perdana Botanical Garden KL's oldest park showcases a variety of native and introduced plants and trees. (p95)

WILAYAH PERSEKUTUAN / LONELY PLANET ©

Best Views

Menara Kuala Lumpur Observe the ring of hills around KL from this telecommunications tower. (p26)

Petronas Towers Watch fearless window cleaners from the 86th-floor observation deck. (p24)

Thean Hou Temple City panoramas and decorative dragons and phoenixes. (p115)

Heli Lounge Bar Bottoms up at the cocktail bar on the helipad. (p40)

Chin Woo Stadium Peaceful Chinatown spot to view sunset across the city. (p70)

Best **Museums & Galleries**

KL has a rich museum and gallery scene, with a large number of excellent small venues, and one or two outstanding collections in the larger museums. With the exception of the Islamic Arts Museum, all are focused on the details of Malaysian life, culture and history, or the creative works of native talents.

Contemporary Art in KL

Malaysia has an impressive contemporary-art scene and KL is the best place to access it, both at public galleries and in several private collections that are open to visitors by appointment.

Among the most interesting and internationally successful contemporary Malaysian artists are Jalaini Abu Hassan ('Jai'), Wong Hoy Cheong, landscape painter Wong Perng Fey and Australian-trained multimedia artist Yee I-Lann. Amron Omar has focused for nearly 30 years on *silat* (a Malay martial art) as a source of inspiration for his paintings, a couple of which hang in the National Visual Arts Gallery in KL.

Latiff Mohidin, who is also a poet, is a Penang-based artist whose work spans several decades and has featured in a major retrospective at the National Visual Arts Gallery; he's considered a national treasure.

Abdul Multhalib Musa's sculptures have won awards; he created several pieces in Beijing for the 2008 Olympics. One of Musa's rippling steel-tube creations can be spotted outside Wisma Selangor Dredging, 142C Jln Ampang, in KL.

☑ Top Tips

▶ Most museums and galleries are free or inexpensive.

▶ The galleries that are located at Publika mall (p48) are a good place to see (and purchase) contemporary oil paintings.

Best for Arts & Crafts

Islamic Arts Museum Marvel at gorgeous works of art inspired by the Muslim faith. (p96)

National Textiles Museum Admire skilful weaving, embroidery, knitting and batik printing. (p62)

Muzium Kraf Small but informative exhibits of

Left: Entrance to the Royal Museum; Above: National Museum

traditional crafts such as wood carvings, metalwork and batik. (p34)

Museum of Ethnic Arts An outstanding private collection filled with tribal and ethnic arts, from Sarawakan masks to Qing dynasty dragon robes. (p70)

Best for History

National Museum Covering the region's history from prehistoric times to the present day. (p102)

Royal Museum A look inside the former Istana Negara (Royal Palace). (p102)

Royal Malaysian Police Museum Excellent small museum that explores the history of Malaysia through the story of policing. (p105)

KL City Gallery Kickstart your understanding of KL. (p62)

Best for Contemporary Art

National Visual Arts Gallery KL's top public gallery, with permanent and temporary collections. (p78)

ILHAM Hosts changing exhibitions that showcase modern and contemporary Malaysian art. (p32)

Galeri Petronas Interesting exhibitions at this great space in Suria KLCC mall. (p33)

Bank Negara Malaysia Museum & Art Gallery Off-the-beaten-track collection of the work of major Malaysian artists. (p78)

Worth a Trip

The excellent **Muzium Orang Asli** (www.jakao.gov. my; 24 Jln Pahang, Gombak; admission free; ⏰9am-5pm Sat-Thu) is dedicated to Peninsular Malaysia's indigenous peoples. Exhibits over two floors highlight the 18 tribes' different traditions, beliefs and cultures. A visit to the museum can be combined with a trip to nearby Batu Caves.

Wei-Ling Gallery One of the city's top private galleries is happy to welcome curious browsers. (p113)

Best
Spas & Wellness

KL stands out among other Southeast Asian cities for having some truly fine spas. And being such a multicultural city, you're as likely to find a Swedish massage place as a fish-nibbling foot spa, Moroccan-style bathhouse or Chinese *tuina* clinic where you can have your troubles kneaded away.

Treatments

Spas offer a wide range of services, from a simple head and shoulder massage to a full package that includes skin scrubbing, steam baths and body wraps. Cheap foot and body massages can be found around Jln Alor, while most shopping malls will have a higher-end massage, spa and beauty clinic.

Exercise

KLites are becoming more active these days, and gyms and yoga classes are easy to find, as are hiking, cycling and other outdoor activity clubs.

Best Spas, Massages, Wellness & Fitness

Spa Village Relaxing pool area and top-class treatments at the Ritz-Carlton. (p32)

Hammam Spa Moroccan tiles, steam baths and scrubs come to KL. (p117)

Donna Spa Balinese-style treatments at the Starhill Gallery. (p34)

Eu Yan Sang This traditional Chinese medicine clinic offers *tuina* massage and scraping therapies for heat exhaustion. (p51)

Buddhist Maha Vihara Meditation classes at a Buddhist temple. (p99)

Chin Woo Stadium Old but good community fitness centre with a big swimming pool. (p70)

Survival Guide

Survival Guide

Before You Go

When to Go

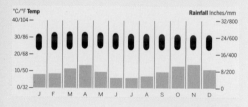

°C/°F Temp
40/104 —
30/86 —
20/68 —
10/50 —
0/32 —

Rainfall Inches/mm
— 32/800
— 24/600
— 16/400
— 8/200
— 0

J F M A M J J A S O N D

➡ **Dry Season (Jan–Feb)** Generally dry with hot days and cooler nights. Busy tourist season with Chinese New Year and Hindu Thaipusam festival.

➡ **Wet Season (Mar–May)** Expect heavy afternoon monsoon showers and slow traffic.

➡ **Dry Season (Jun–Sep)** Driest and hottest time of the year and most touristed. Especially popular with Middle Eastern travellers July and August. Enjoy fresh durians June to August.

➡ **Wet Season (Oct–Dec)** Another rainy season with heavy afternoon showers. Tourist numbers lower and nights are pleasant.

Book Your Stay

➡ KLites' love of brands is reflected in the city's many international hotel chains.

➡ You can often grab great online deals for top-end accommodation, and there are also some excellent new boutique-style midrange options.

➡ Budget sleeps are plentiful, too, but the best places fill up quickly, so book ahead – especially over public holidays.

➡ Some of KL's best accommodation deals, particularly for longer stays, are offered by serviced apartments.

Useful Websites

iBilik (www.ibilik.my) Room rentals in Malaysia.

Asia Homestay (www.asiahomestay.com) Malaysian homestay booking site.

Lonely Planet (www.lonelyplanet.com/

alaysia/kuala-lumpur/
otels) Recommenda-
ons and bookings.

est Budget

ackHome (www.
ackhome.com.my)
tripped-back concrete-
nic dorms and rooms,
lus a great cafe.

antern Hotel (www.
anternhotel.com) Slick,
ontemporary hotel in
ne heart of Chinatown.

Reggae Mansion (www.
eggaehostelsmalaysia.
om/mansion) Cool
rash pad for the modern
backpacker.

Best Midrange

**Sekeping Teng-
giri** (www.sekeping.com)
Rough-luxe guesthouse
with ace contemporary-
art gallery thrown in.

Kuala Lumpur Journal
(www.kljournalhotel.com)
Hip new boutique hotel
in Bukit Bintang with a
fantastic rooftop pool.

**Aloft Kuala Lumpur
Sentral** (www.starwood-
hotels.com/alofthotels)
Playful, relaxed concept
hotel steps from the KLIA
Express.

Best Top End

Majestic Hotel (www.
majestickl.com) Heritage
hotel with a modern
tower wing and a gor-
geous spa.

G Tower Hotel (www.
gtowerhotel.com) Slick,
modern luxury accom-
modation on the upper
floors of the G Tower.

Villa Samadhi (www.
villasamadhi.com.my)
Beautiful Asian-chic
bolthole with gorgeous
tree-shaded pool.

Arriving in Kuala Lumpur

Kuala Lumpur International Airport

➡ **Kuala Lumpur Interna-
tional Airport** (KLIA; ☎03-
8777 7000; www.klia.com.my;
🚇KLIA), which comprises
two terminals, is about
55km south of the city.

➡ The fastest way to the
city is on the comfortable
KLIA Ekspres (☎03-2278

9009; www.kliaekspres.
com; adult/child one way
RM55/25), with departures
every 15 to 20 minutes
from 5am to 1am. From
KL Sentral you can
transfer to your final destination by monorail, light
rail (LRT), KTM Komuter
train or taxi.

➡ The **Airport Coach**
(☎016-228 9070; www.
airportcoach.com.my; one
way/return RM10/18) takes
an hour to KL Sentral; for
RM18 it will take you to
any central KL hotel from
KLIA and pick you up for
the return journey for
RM25. The bus stand is
clearly signposted inside
the terminal. Other bus
companies connecting
KLIA to KL Sentral are
Skybus (☎016-217 6950;
www.skybus.com.my; one way
RM10) and **Aerobus** (☎03
3344 8828; www.aerobus.my;
one way RM9).

➡ Taxis from KLIA oper-
ate both on a fixed-fare
coupon system and the
meter. Buy your taxi
coupon before you exit
the arrivals hall; standard
taxis cost RM75 (for up
to three people), premier
taxis for four people
RM103 and family-sized
minivans seating up to
eight RM200. The journey
will take around one hour.

SkyPark Subang

➡ Firefly and Berjaya Air flights land at **SkyPark Subang Airport** (Sultan Abdul Aziz Shah Airport; ☏03-7842 2773; www.subangskypark.com; M17, Subang), around 20km west of the city centre.

➡ **Trans MVS Express** (☏019-307 2521; www.facebook.com/Transmvsexpress) offers on-the-hour services from KL Sentral to Skypark Subang (RM10, one hour) between 9am and 9pm; and from Skypark Subang to KLIA and KLIA2 (RM10, one hour) roughly every two hours between 5am and 11pm.

➡ Taxis charge around RM40 to RM50 into the city, depending on traffic, which can be heavy during rush hour.

KL Sentral

➡ All long-distance trains depart from KL Sentral, hub of the **KTM** (Keretapi Tanah Melayu Berhad; ☏03-2267 1200; www.ktmb.com.my; ☉call centre 7am-10pm) national railway system. The information office in the main hall can advise on schedules and check seat availability.

➡ There are daily connections with Butterworth,

Wakaf Baharu (for Kota Bharu and Jerantut), Johor Bahru, Thailand and Singapore; fares are cheap, especially if you opt for a seat rather than a berth (for which there are extra charges), but journey times are slow.

➡ KL Sentral runs a coupon system for taxis – look for the counters near the exits from the KLIA Ekspres/Transit lines and main KTM/KTM Komuter lines.

Terminal Bersepadu Selatan

➡ Connected to the Bandar Tasik Selatan train-station hub, about 15 minutes south of KL Sentral, is **Terminal Bersepadu Selatan** (TBS; ☏03-9051 2000; www.tbsbts.com.my; Jln Terminal Selatan, Bandar Tasik Selatan; Ⓜ Bandar Tasik Seletan, Ⓡ Bandar Tasik Seletan). Built to replace Pudu Sentral as KL's main long-distance bus station, TBS serves destinations to the south and northeast of KL. This vast, modern transport hub has a centralised ticketing service (CTS) selling tickets for nearly all bus companies – including services offered by major

operator **Transnasional Express** (☏03-9051 2000; www.transnasional.com.my; Terminal Bersepadu Selatan Jln Terminal Selatan, Bandar Tasik Selatan) – at counter on level 3 or online (up to three hours before departure).

Getting Around

LRT, Monorail, Komuter Train & MRT

➡ Rapid KL runs the **Light Rail Transit** (LRT; ☏03-7885 2585; www.myrapid.com.my; from RM1.30; ☉every 6-10min 6am-11.45pm Mon-Sat, to 11.30pm Sun) system. There are three lines: the Ampang line from Ampang to Sentul Timur; the Sri Petaling line from Sentul Timur to Putra Heights; and the Kelana Jaya line from Gombak to Putra Heights. It's handy (for Chinatown, Kampung Baru, KLCC), but the network is poorly integrated.

➡ The air-conditioned **monorail** (www.myrapid.com.my; RM1.20-4.10;

(6am-midnight) zips from _ Sentral to Titiwangsa, king many of the city's ightseeing areas.

KTM Komuter (www. mb.com.my; from RM1.40; 6.45am-11.45pm) train ervices run every 15 to 0 minutes and use KL entral as a hub. There e two lines: Tanjung lalim–Sungai Gadut and atu Caves–Pelabuhan lang.

The Klang Valley **Mass apid Transit (MRT) roject** (www.mymrt. om.my) involves the reation of three new ommuter rail lines, the rst of which is the 51km ungai Buloh–Kajang ne. Phase one, from ungai Buloh to Seman-an, was completed in ate 2016. The remaining part of the line to Kajang will be finished the follow-ng year.

Tourist Buses

The **GOKL free city bus** (1800-887 723; www. facebook.com/goklcitybus; 6am-11pm Mon-Thu, to 1am Sat, 7am-11pm Sun) has four circular routes around the city, with stops at KLCC, KL Tower, KL Sentral, the National Museum and Merdeka Sq. Buses run

every five minutes during peak hours and every 10 to 15 minutes at other times.

The double-decker, air-con **Hop-On Hop-Off** (03-9282 2713; www. myhoponhopoff.com; adult/ child 24hr ticket RM45/24; 9am-7pm) bus makes a circuit of the main tourist sites half-hourly through-out the day and can be a handy way to get around, if you avoid rush hour.

Taxi

KL has plenty of air conditioned taxis, which queue at designated taxi stops across the city. You can also flag down moving taxis, but drivers will stop only if there is a convenient place to pull over.

Fares start at RM3 for the first three minutes, with an additional 25 sen for each 36 seconds.

From midnight to 6am there's a surcharge of 50% on the metered fare, and extra passengers (more than two) add 20 sen each to the starting fare.

Blue taxis are newer and more comfortable and start at RM6 for the first three minutes and RM1 for each addi-tional 36 seconds. Night surcharges of 50% also apply.

Unfortunately, some drivers have limited geographical knowledge of the city. Some also refuse to use the meter, even though this is a legal requirement.

Note that KL Sentral and some large malls such as Pavilion and Su-ria KLCC have a coupon system for taxis where you pay in advance at a slightly higher fee than the meter.

Tickets & Passes

Rapid KL offers the **MyRapid** (www.myrapid. com.my) pre-paid card, valid on Rapid KL buses, the monorail and LRT lines.

The **Touch 'n Go card** (www.touchngo.com. my) can be used on all public transport.

For short-term stays you are better off buying individual tickets.

→ One of the easiest ways to use taxis in KL is to download an app such as **Uber**, **Easy Taxi** or **Grab** (formally known as My Teksi) to your smartphone or tablet.

Essential Information

Business Hours

Banks 10am to 3pm Monday to Friday, 9.30am to 11.30am Saturday

Restaurants noon to 2.30pm and 6pm to 10.30pm

Shops 9.30am to 7pm Monday to Saturday, malls 10am to 10pm daily

Discount Cards

The new **KL Pass** (adult/child one-day pass RM165/125, three-day pass RM395/325, six-day pass RM675/515) includes free or discounted entry to a number of the city's attractions, including the Aquaria KLCC and KL Tower, as well as unlimited rides on the KL

hop-on, hop-off bus. It can save you money, but you'll need to squeeze in trips to a few different attractions to make it worthwhile.

Electricity

240V/50Hz

Emergency

Police & Ambulance ☏999

Fire ☏994

Tourist Police ☏03-9235 4999

Money

Most hotels and restaurants accept credit cards. ATMs are widely available.

ATMs & Credit Cards

MasterCard and Visa are the most widely accepted brands of credit card. You can make ATM withdrawals with your PIN, or banks such as Maybank (Malaysia's biggest bank), HSBC and Standard Chartered will accept credit cards for over-the-counter cash advances. Many banks are also linked to international banking networks such as Cirrus (the most common), Maestro and Plus, allowing withdrawals from overseas savings or chequing accounts.

Contact details for credit-card companies in Malaysia:

American Express (www.americanexpress.com/malaysia)

Diners Card (www.diners.com.my)

MasterCard (www.mastercard.com/sea)

Visa (www.visa-asia.com)

Tipping

Giving a tip is not generally expected, but leaving small change in a cafe or restaurant is appreciated. A service charge of around 10% will be added onto the bill in many restaurants.

blic Holidays

well as fixed secular idays, various religious tivals (which change es annually) are tional holidays. These lude Chinese New ar (in January/Febru-y), the Hindu festival of epavali (in October/ ovember), the Buddhist stival of Wesak (April/ ay) and the Muslim stivals of Hari Raya Haji, ari Raya Puasa, Mawlid -Nabi and Awal Muhar-m (Muslim New Year).

Fixed annual holidays clude the following:

ew Year's Day
January

ederal Territory Day
February (KL and Putra-ya only)

ultan of Selangor's irthday Second Satur-ay in March (Selangor nly)

abour Day 1 May

Yang di-Pertuan Ag-ong's (King's) Birthday First Saturday in June

National Day (Hari Ke-bangsaan) 31 August

Christmas Day
25 December

Managing Kuala Lumpur's Many Holidays

Malaysia has a full roster of public holidays and during Ramadan, Deepavali and Chinese New Year there is a festive atmosphere about town, much like Christmas in the West. Be aware that hotels and transport can be booked solid, and restaurants, banks, museums and other tourist attractions closed during these times. ATMs may also be short on cash. The city never entirely shuts down, and when one ethnic group is off celebrating, another will usually take up the slack. During Chinese New Year, for example, many Chinese go to Little India to eat.

Safe Travel

➡ KL is generally very safe, but watch for pickpockets on crowded public transport.

➡ Theft and violence are not particularly common in Malaysia. However, muggings and bag snatches do happen and physical attacks have been known to occur, particularly after hours and in rundown areas of KL.

➡ Thieves on motorbikes target women for grab raids on their handbags; where possible walk against the direction of traffic and carry your bag over the arm that's furthest from the road.

➡ Be wary of demonstrations, particularly over religious or ethnic issues, as these can turn violent.

➡ Use credit cards only at established businesses and guard your credit-card numbers closely.

➡ Carry a small, sturdy padlock you can use for cheap hotel-room doors and hostel lockers, and to keep prying fingers out of your bags in left-luggage rooms.

➡ One ongoing irritation is the state of the pavements. The covers thrown over drains can give way suddenly, so walk around them.

Telephone

Local SIM cards can be used in most mobile phones; if not, set your phone to roaming.

If you have arranged global roaming with your home provider, your GSM digital phone will automatically tune in to one of the region's digital networks. If not, buy a prepaid SIM card for one of the local networks on arrival. The rate for a local call is around 40 sen per minute. There are three mobile-phone companies, all with similar call rates and prepaid packages:

Celcom (www.celcom.com.my)

DiGi (www.digi.com.my)

Maxis (www.maxis.com.my)

Toilets

➡ Western-style sit-down loos are now the norm, but there are still a few places with Asian squat toilets.

➡ Toilet paper is often not provided; instead, you will find a hose or a spout on the toilet seat, which you are supposed to use as a bidet, or a bucket of water and a tap.

Tourist Informati~~on~~

➡ **Tourism Malaysia** (www.tourismmalaysia. gov.my) has a network of domestic offices that are good for brochures and free maps but rathe~~r~~ weak on hard factual information. Its oversea~~s~~ offices are useful for predeparture planning. There are regional office~~s~~ in Kuala Lumpur.

➡ In addition to supplyin~~g~~ tons of useful brochures and maps, **Visit KL** (Kual~~a~~ Lumpur Tourism Bureau; ☏03-2698 0332; www. visitkl.gov.my; 11 Jln Tangsi; ⏰8.30am-5.30pm Mon-Fri; 🛜; Ⓜ Masjid Jamek) runs four excellent free walking tours.

Travellers with Disabilities

For the mobility impaired~~,~~ Kuala Lumpur can be a nightmare. There are often no footpaths, kerbs can be very high, construction sites are everywhere, and crossings are few and far between.

Before setting off, get in touch with your national support organisation (preferably with the travel officer, if there is one). Download Lonely Planet's free Accessible Travel guide from

Dos & Don'ts

Malaysians are generally very polite and dislike confrontation, and you'd do well to bear in mind the following points of etiquette:

Keep calm Try to avoid raising your voice in anger. A dispute is more likely to be resolved through calm discussion, and a smile often goes a long way.

Greetings Handshakes are usual when meeting someone for the first time, although some Muslims prefer not to shake hands with someone of the opposite sex.

Pointing Don't use your index finger to point; use your thumb instead.

Shoes off Always remove your footwear before entering someone's home.

Right handed Use your right hand to eat, in shops, when shaking hands or for any other transaction. The left hand is reserved for unclean acts.

p://lptravel.to/Acces-
leTravel for travel tips
d resources. Also try
e following:

cessible Journeys
ww.disabilitytravel.
m) In the US.

**bility International
SA** (www.miusa.org) In
e US.

can (www.nican.com.
) In Australia.

Tourism for All (www.
tourismforall.org.uk) In
the UK.

Visas

➡ Visitors must have a
passport valid for at least
six months beyond the
date of entry. You may
also be asked to provide
proof of a ticket for on-

ward travel and sufficient
funds to cover your stay.

➡ Only under special
circumstances can Israeli
citizens enter Malaysia.

➡ Nationals of most other
countries are given a 30-,
60- or 90-day visa on
arrival. Full details of visa
requirements are avail-
able at www.kln.gov.my.

Language

The official language of Kuala Lumpur is Malay, or Bahasa Malaysia, as it's called by its speakers. It is very similar to Indonesian.

Malay pronunciation is easy to master. Each letter always represents the same sound and most letters are pronounced the same as their English counterparts, with *c* pronounced as the 'ch' in 'chat' and *sy* as the 'sh' in 'ship'. Note also that *kh* is a guttural sound (like the 'ch' in the Scottish *loch*), and that *gh* is a throaty 'g' sound.

To enhance your trip with a phrasebook, visit **lonelyplanet.com**. Lonely Planet iPhone phrasebooks are available through the Apple App store.

Basics

Hello.	*Helo.*
Goodbye.	
(by person leaving)	*Selamat tinggal.*
(by person staying)	*Selamat jalan.*
Yes.	*Ya.*
No.	*Tidak.*
Please.	*Tolong.*
Thank you.	*Terima kasih.*
You're welcome.	*Sama-sama.*
Excuse me.	*Maaf.*
Sorry.	*Minta maaf.*
How are you?	*Apa khabar?*
Fine, thanks.	*Khabar baik.*

Do you speak English?
Bolehkah anda berbicara Bahasa Inggeris?

I don't understand.
Saya tidak faham.

Eating & Drinking

Can I see the menu?
Minta senarai makanan?

I'd like ... *Saya mahu...*

I'm a vegetarian.
Saya makan sayur-sayuran sahaja.

Not too spicy, please.
Kurang pedas.

Please add extra chilli.
Tolong letak cili lebih.

Thank you, that was delicious.
Sedap sekali, terima kasih.

Please bring the bill.
Tolong bawa bil.

Shopping

I'd like to buy ...	*Saya nak beli ...*
I'm just looking.	*Saya nak tengok saja*

Can I look at it?
Boleh saya lihat barang itu?

I don't like it.	*Saya tak suka ini.*
How much is it?	*Berapa harganya?*
It's too expensive.	*Mahalnya.*

Can you lower the price?
Boleh kurang sedikit?

Emergencies

Help!	*Tolong!*
Go away!	*Pergi!*
I'm lost.	*Saya sesat.*

There's been an accident.
Ada kemalangan.

Call a doctor!	*Panggil doktor!*
Call the police!	*Panggil polis!*

n ill. *Saya sakit.*

hurts here. *Sini sakit.*

m allergic to (antibiotics).
aya alergik kepada (antibiotik).

andas Toilets

ime & Numbers

What time is it? *Pukul berapa?*

t's (seven) o'clock. *Pukul (tujuh).*

alf past (one). *Pukul (satu) setengah.*

n the morning *pagi*

n the afternoon *tengahari*

n the evening *petang*

esterday *semalam*

oday *hari ini*

omorrow *esok*

Monday *hari Isnin*

Tuesday *hari Selasa*

Wednesday *hari Rabu*

Thursday *hari Khamis*

Friday *hari Jumaat*

Saturday *hari Sabtu*

Sunday *hari Minggu*

1	satu
2	dua
3	tiga
4	empat
5	lima
6	cnam
7	tujuh
8	lapan
9	sembilan
10	sepuluh
20	dua puluh
30	tiga puluh
40	empat puluh
50	lima puluh
60	enam puluh
70	tujuh puluh
80	lapan puluh
90	sembilan puluh
100	seratus
1000	seribu

Transport & Directions

I want to go to ... *Saya nak ke ...*

What time does the (bus) leave?
(Bas) bertolak pukul berapa?

What time does the (train) arrive?
(Keretapi) tiba pukul berapa?

Can you tell me when we get to ...?
*Tolong beritahu saya bila kita sudah
sampai di ...?*

I want to get off at ...
Saya nak turun di ...

bicycle-rickshaw *beca*

boat *bot*

bus *bas*

plane *kapal terbang*

ship *kapal*

taxi *teksi*

train *keretapi*

Where is ...? *Di mana ...?*

What's the address? *Apakah alamatnya?*

Can you write the address, please?
Tolong tuliskan alamat itu?

Can you show me (on the map)?
Tolong tunjukkan (di pcta)?

Go straight ahead. *Jalan terus.*

Turn left. *Belok kiri.*

Turn right. *Belok kanan.*

Behind the Scenes

Send Us Your Feedback

We love to hear from travellers – your comments help make our books better. We read every word, and we guarantee that your feedback goes straight to the authors. Visit **lonelyplanet.com/contact** to submit your updates and suggestions.

Note: We may edit, reproduce and incorporate your comments in Lonely Planet products such as guidebooks, websites and digital products, so let us know if you don't want your comments reproduced or your name acknowledged. For a copy of our privacy policy visit lonelyplanet.com/privacy.

Our Readers

Many thanks to the travellers, Catarina Selbekk and Jacqui Wood, who used the last edition and wrote to us with helpful hints, useful advice and interesting anecdotes.

Isabel's Thanks

Huge thanks to Simon Richmond for his help and advice and to Alex Yong for his cheerful assistance with so much of my research. *Terima kasih*, also, to Noraza Yusof, Jane Rai, Scott Dunn and Ana Abdullah. For their company on the road and research tips, thanks to Kevin Chong, Siddiq Sulaiman Zainal Azhar, Fazal Mahbob, Farrah Aqlima, Matt Hobbins and Helen Armstrong.

Acknowledgements

Cover photograph: Thean Hou Temple, Kuala Lumpur, Gavin Hellier/AWL ©
Contents photograph: Sultan Abdul Samad Building, Kuala Lumpur, Tom Bonaventure/Getty ©

This Book

This 2nd edition of Lonely Planet's *Pocket Kuala Lumpur* guidebook was researched and written by Isabel Albiston. The previous edition was researched and written by Robert Kelly. This guidebook was produced by the following:

Destination Editors
Lauren Keith, Sarah Reid

Product Editor
Kate Mathews

Senior Cartographer
Julie Sheridan

Book Designer Jessica Rose

Assisting Editors Sarah Bailey, Imogen Bannister, Carolyn Boicos, Victoria Harrison, Gabrielle Stefanos

Cover Researcher
Naomi Parker

Thanks to Liz Heynes, Catherine Naghten, Dora Whitaker, Tracy Whitmey, Juan Winata

Sights 000
Map Pages **000**

SORINA CHIRITA

LONELY PLANET IN THE WILD

Send your 'Lonely Planet in the Wild' photos to social@lonelyplanet.com
We share the best on our Facebook page every week!

Our Writer

Isabel Albiston

After six years working for the *Daily Telegraph* in London, squeezing in as many trips as annual leave would allow, Isabel left to spend more time on the road. Isabel started writing for Lonely Planet in 2014. Travel highlights include reporting on the flamingos of Tanzania's Lake Natron, mountain biking in Bolivia, horse riding across the Atacama Desert in Chile, visiting a sweat lodge in Mexico, eating a sushi breakfast at Tsukiji Market in Tokyo, ice skating on a frozen pond in St Petersburg, walking the Camino de Santiago in Spain, hiking in the Kelabit Highlands in Sarawak, Malaysia, and travelling overland from Singapore to Nepal via China, Tibet and Everest base camp. See her pics on instagram: isabel_albiston.

Published by Lonely Planet Global Limited
CRN 554153
2nd edition – June 2017
ISBN 978 1 78657 534 0
© Lonely Planet 2017   Photographs © as indicated 2017
10 9 8 7 6 5 4 3 2 1
Printed in China